Land Law

Cavendish
Publishing
Limited

First published in Great Britain 1997 by Cavendish Publishing Limited, The Glass House, Wharton Street, London WC1X 9PX.

Telephone: 0171-278 8000 Facsimile: 0171-278 8080

Lawcard on land law

1.Land tenure - Law and legislation – England
2.Land tenure - Law and legislation – England - Examinations, questions, etc.
I.Land Law
344.2'0643

ISBN 1 85941 321 8

Printed and bound in Great Britain

Contents

1 General principles and estates

Definition of land

This is given in s 205(1)(ix) of the LPA 1925:

'... land of any tenure and mines and minerals, whether or not held apart from the surface, buildings or parts of buildings (whether the division is horizontal, vertical or made in any other way) and other corporeal hereditaments; also a manor, an advowson, and a rent and other incorporeal hereditaments, and an easement, right, privilege, or benefit in, over or derived from land.'

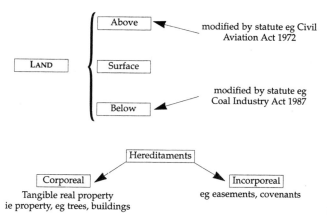

Fixtures and fittings

A purchaser is entitled to fixtures but not to fittings. Fixtures are determined by the two-pronged test in *Holland v Hodgson* (1872)

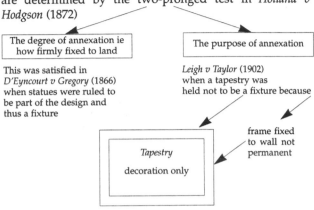

The degree of annexation ie how firmly fixed to land

This was satisfied in *D'Eyncourt v Gregory* (1866) when statues were ruled to be part of the design and thus a fixture

The purpose of annexation

Leigh v Taylor (1902) when a tapestry was held not to be a fixture because

frame fixed to wall not permanent

Tapestry

decoration only

Estates: the 1925 legislation

Section 1(1) of the LPA 1925 reduced these to two only:

An estate in fee simple absolute in possession

An estate for a term of absolute

Absolute means no conditions

Possession is defined in s 205(1)(xix) of the LPA 1925 as in 'receipt of rents and profits or right to receive same, if any'.

There are some estates regarded as 'freehold' which do not come within these two legal estates. For example:

Determinable fee simple	Conditional fee simple
1 Ends with a specified event	Two forms:
2 The specified event need never occur	a) Condition precedent where the condition must be fulfilled before the estate can be vested in the grantee
3 Words such as until, during, while, as long as	b) Condition subsequent where the fee simple is vested but subsequently determines because the conditioning event occurs
4 If the specified event occurs the estate reverts to the grantor unless it is a school, church, museum etc when under Revertor of Sites Act 1987 it becomes subject to a trust for sale with the grantor and his successors in title, the beneficiaries	

Other interests in land

Legal interests are listed in s 1(2) of the LPA 1925 as:

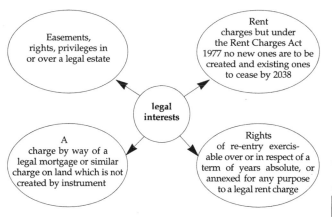

Section 7 of the LPA 1925 was amended by the LP (Amendment) Act 1926 to include as legal estates within s 1(1) LPA 1925 estates subject to a rent charge payment condition so that they are now fee simple absolute in possession estates.

All other interests are equitable.

2 Unregistered land: the doctrine of notice and the Land Charges Acts 1925 and 1972

The doctrine of notice

Legal rights are rights *in rem* so that they are good against the whole world. Equitable rights are not. Before 1926 equitable rights were subject to the doctrine of notice so that a purchaser was only bound by them if he had, or could have had, notice of them.

Interests which are not subject to registration under the Land Charges Acts for unregistered land are still subject to this doctrine of notice.

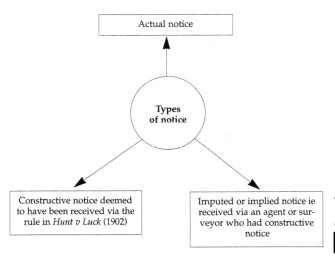

Actual notice

Types of notice

Constructive notice deemed to have been received via the rule in *Hunt v Luck* (1902)

Imputed or implied notice ie received via an agent or surveyor who had constructive notice

The rule in *Hunt v Luck* (1902): a purchaser must make sufficient and correct enquiries. If he could have discovered an interest had he done so, he is deemed to have had constructive notice of it.

Example: *Kingsnorth Finance Trust Co v Tizzard* (1986).

A husband and wife were separated but W stayed in the matrimonial home when H was away, and came every morning to see the children to school and also came to give them meals.	W had an equitable interest in the house but the legal title was in H's name only. H took out a mortgage telling the company that his wife no longer lived there.

The mortgage company sent a surveyor to look at the house and check the wife was not in occupation. He reported back that the house was occupied only by H and his children.	**Held**: The company had imputed notice of the wife's occupation because had the surveyor looked in the wardrobe he would have seen evidence of her occupation. The surveyor had constructive notice of her occupation under the rule in *Hunt v Luck*.

Result
Since the company had imputed notice of the wife's interest, they should have paid the money to two trustees, not to H alone, so W's interest was not overreached and the company was bound by it.

Overreachable interests

Overreachable interests are beneficial interests which a purchaser is not concerned with if he pays the purchase money to two trustees.

They arise where there is a settlement subject to either the LPA 1925 or the SLA 1925.

Overreachable interests

A trust for sale

Interests here are in money as soon the trust is created under the doctrine of conversion and are overreached if the purchase money is paid to two trustees: s 27 LPA 1925.

A strict settlement

The beneficiaries' interests are in the capital sum raised on sale but are overreached if the purchase money is paid to two trustees: s 18 SLA 1925.

See Settlements, Chapter 5.

The Land Charges Act 1972

This applies to unregistered land only. The most important charges are:

Class C land charges

Class C(i) *Puisne* mortgage ie mortgage not protected by deposit of title deeds.

Class C(ii) Limited owner charge, eg put on register by a tenant for life.

Class C(iii) A general equitable charge.

Class C(iv) An estate contract.

Class D land charges

Class D(i) an Inland Revenue charge when inheritance tax is outstanding.

Class D(ii) restrictive covenants created after 1 January 1926.

Class D (iii) Equitable easements created after 1 January 1926.

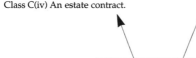

the most important land charges

The MHA 1983 created a further land charge.

Class F land Charges
A spouse's right of occupation of the matrimonial home under MHA 1983.

Problems associated with land charges

Registration
Interests are registered in the name of owner affected by that interest, which may not be known particularly where land is leased: *Diligent Finance Co Ltd v Alleyne* (1972); *White v Bijou Mansions* (1937)

Class C(iv)
Estate contracts include contracts for sale, options to purchase, rights of pre-emption. When more than one is registered, which has priority?: *Pritchard v Briggs* (1980)

PROBLEMS

Class D(iii)
Shiloh Spinners v Harding (1973) A right of re-entry was ruled by the House of Lords not to be registrable as an equitable interest, but subject to the doctrine of notice

Priority of interests
The equitable maxim 'where the priorities are equal, the first in time prevails', applies **but** here this means the first to be **created** not the first to be registered

The problem of estate contracts

Pritchard v Briggs (1990)

An estate contract
ie an option to purchase

An estate contract
ie a right of pre-emption

Which had priority?

Answer:
The option to purchase.
The pre-emption will never have priority because it is a mere *spes*.

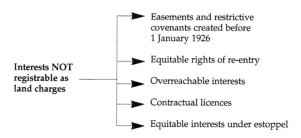

Interests NOT registrable as land charges

- Easements and restrictive covenants created before 1 January 1926
- Equitable rights of re-entry
- Overreachable interests
- Contractual licences
- Equitable interests under estoppel

What happens if a registrable interest is not registered?

Sections 4(2) and (5) mean that where an interest has not been registered it is void against a purchaser of the charged land.

It does not matter if the purchaser knew of the interest or not: *Midland Bank Trust Co v Green* (1981) illustrated below.

Midland Bank Trust Co v Green (1981)

A father gives his son an option to purchase his farm

⬇

When father and son quarrel, the son leaves the farm

⬇

The father then sells the farm to his wife for £1

⬇

The wife then dies

⬇

The son now tries to exercise his option to purchase

⬇

The court rules that he cannot do so. He had failed to register his option as a Class C(iv) land charge

⬇

It did not matter that his mother knew of his father's grant of the option, nor that she only paid a nominal sum for the farm

3   Land registration

Aims and principles

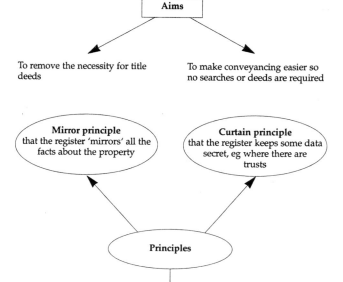

Aims

To remove the necessity for title deeds

To make conveyancing easier so no searches or deeds are required

Mirror principle
that the register 'mirrors' all the facts about the property

Curtain principle
that the register keeps some data secret, eg where there are trusts

Principles

Insurance principle
that the state guarantees the register is correct

The registers

There are, in fact, three registers

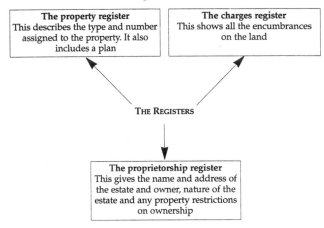

The property register
This describes the type and number assigned to the property. It also includes a plan

The charges register
This shows all the encumbrances on the land

THE REGISTERS

The proprietorship register
This gives the name and address of the estate and owner, nature of the estate and any property restrictions on ownership

What the owner receives

The owner receives a **Land Certificate** which replaces the title deeds and indicates which title the land has been given:

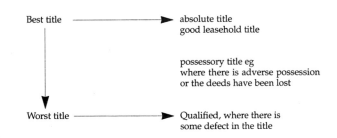

Best title ⟶ absolute title
good leasehold title

possessory title eg
where there is adverse possession or the deeds have been lost

Worst title ⟶ Qualified, where there is some defect in the title

The protection of interests

Minor interests are protected in four ways:

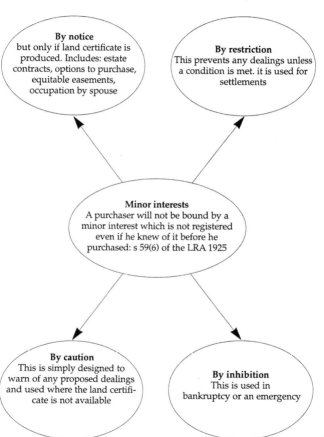

By notice
but only if land certificate is produced. Includes: estate contracts, options to purchase, equitable easements, occupation by spouse

By restriction
This prevents any dealings unless a condition is met. it is used for settlements

Minor interests
A purchaser will not be bound by a minor interest which is not registered even if he knew of it before he purchased: s 59(6) of the LRA 1925

By caution
This is simply designed to warn of any proposed dealings and used where the land certificate is not available

By inhibition
This is used in bankruptcy or an emergency

Problems

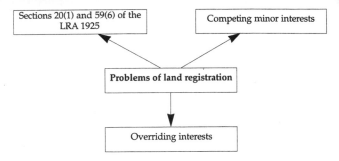

Sections 20(1) and 59(6) of the LRA 1925

Section 20(1). Minor interests which are registered are protected; unregistered interests are void against a purchaser.

Section 59(6). A purchaser takes free of any unregistered interest whether he had notice of it or not, and whether the notice was actual, implied or constructive notice.

This is illustrated by *Peffer v Rigg* (1977).

Peffer v Rigg (1977)

Two married couples H1 & W1 and H2 & W2

The matrimonial home of H1 and W1 was purchased with money provided by H1 and H2, but the conveyance was in H1's name only

This gave H2 a beneficial interest under a resulting trust in H1's house

H1 and W1 decide to separate and as part of the separation settlement H1 sells W1 the house for £1. W1 knew that H2 had a beneficial interest in the house

H2 had not registered his interest, so, under s 20(1) his interest was void against a purchaser and s 59(6) even if that purchaser knew of it

BUT

the court ruled when s 20(1) and s 59(6) are read together s 59(6) applies only to a purchaser in good faith which W1 was not

Also see *Lyus v Prowsa* (1982).

Competing minor interests

In equity: where the equities are equal, 'the first in time prevails' so which?

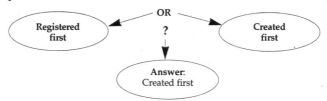

This applies for a notice or caution
authority: *Barclays Bank v Taylor* (1974)
affirmed in *Mortgage Corp v Nationwide Credit Corp* (1993)

Overriding interests: s 70(1) LRA 1925

These are an exception to the mirror principle since they are not registrable.

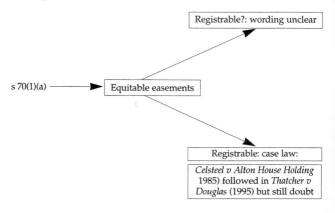

s 70(1)(a) ──► Equitable easements

Registrable?: wording unclear

Registrable: case law:

Celsteel v Alton House Holding 1985) followed in *Thatcher v Douglas* (1995) but still doubt

s 70(1)(g)   '… the rights of every person in occupation.' This means: the right must be in the land itself and the person with the right must be in actual occupation or in receipt of its rents.

A purchaser will not take free of such rights unless he enquired under the rule in *Hunt v Luck* and was not told of those rights.

Cases

Actual occupation:	*William and Glyn's Bank v Boland* (1981)
	An equitable interest and actual occupation gave rise to an overriding interest under s 70(1)(g)
In receipt of rents or profits:	*Strand Securities v Caswell* (1966)
	Occupation by a stepdaughter who did not pay rent did **not** give an overriding interest under s 70(1)(g)

Rectification of the register

There is provision for rectification of mistakes made in the register, under s 82 of the LRA 1925, which allows rectification in eight particular circumstances.

The court has a discretion in the matter but cannot order rectification where this would involve a registered proprietor in possession unless the mistake results from that proprietor, or to give effect to an overriding interest.

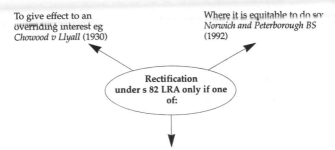

To give effect to an overriding interest eg *Chowood v Llyall* (1930)

Where it is equitable to do so *Norwich and Peterborough BS* (1992)

Rectification under s 82 LRA only if one of:

Where there is fraud or lack of care by the registered proprietor which caused the error

Note

Section 83 of the LRA 1925 allows an indemnity to be paid for loss suffered; but this does not apply to rectification to give effect to an overriding interest as in adverse possession because the interest exists before the rectification takes place.

The recommendations of the Law Commission 1987

Although the Law Commission made several recommendations on registration none have been implemented. The main ones were as follows:

Recommendations on overriding interests

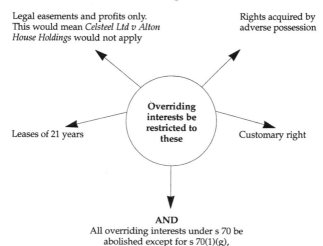

Legal easements and profits only. This would mean *Celsteel Ltd v Alton House Holdings* would not apply

Rights acquired by adverse possession

Overriding interests be restricted to these

Leases of 21 years

Customary right

AND
All overriding interests under s 70 be abolished except for s 70(1)(g), rights by actual occupation

Other recommendations

All other interests to be minor interests only.

Rectification indemnity provision for loss resulting from an overriding interest.

4 Co-ownership and trusts for sale

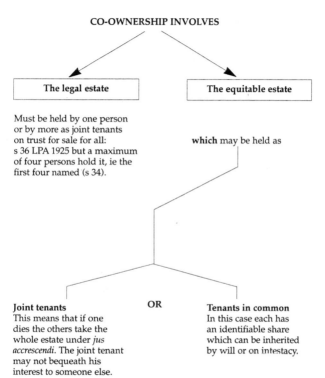

CO-OWNERSHIP INVOLVES

The legal estate

Must be held by one person or by more as joint tenants on trust for sale for all: s 36 LPA 1925 but a maximum of four persons hold it, ie the first four named (s 34).

The equitable estate

which may be held as

Joint tenants
This means that if one dies the others take the whole estate under *jus accrescendi*. The joint tenant may not bequeath his interest to someone else.

OR

Tenants in common
In this case each has an identifiable share which can be inherited by will or on intestacy.

The creation of a legal and equitable joint tenancy

This requires the four unities:

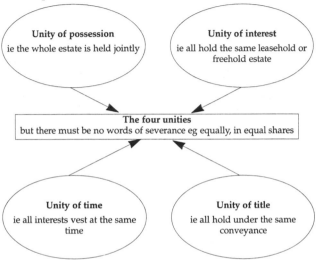

Unity of possession
ie the whole estate is held jointly

Unity of interest
ie all hold the same leasehold or freehold estate

The four unities
but there must be no words of severance eg equally, in equal shares

Unity of time
ie all interests vest at the same time

Unity of title
ie all hold under the same conveyance

'Equity leans against joint tenancies', and presumes a tenancy in common in the following circumstances:

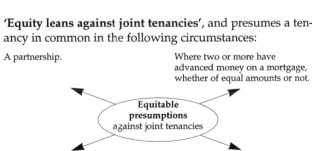

A partnership.

Where two or more have advanced money on a mortgage, whether of equal amounts or not.

Equitable presumptions
against joint tenancies

Where persons are joint legal tenants but provided different contributions to the purchase.

Where ownership is for multiple business purposes. This is a PC decision in *Malaysian Credit Ltd v Jack Chia Mph* (1986), so it is persuasive only.

Severance of an equitable joint tenancy under s 36(2) of the LPA 1925

s 36 LPA 1925

By written notice sent to address of other joint tenant (s 196) even if not received *Re 88 Berkeley Rd, London* (1971)

By 'such other acts'

Meaning of 'such other acts'

Conflicting cases:

Re Drapers Conveyance (1969)
Harris v Goddard (1983)
Hunter v Babbage (1994)

Mutual agreement:

Burgess v Rawnsley (1975)

REMEMBER JOINT TENANCY SEVERED BUT LEGAL ESTATE STILL JOINT

Alienation:

eg selling to a stranger

Bankruptcy:

must be before death:
Re Palmer (1993)

Co-ownership, equity and trusts for sale

A trust for sale is defined in s 205(xxix) of the LPA 1925 as an 'immediate binding trust for sale'.

This means that there is a duty to sell (s 35) and a power to postpone sale (s 25(4)).

Immediately the trust is created the **doctrine of conversion** comes into being and interests are in money and not in land.

Note: Under the Trusts of Land and Appointment of Trustees Act 1996, the doctrine of conversion will cease to exist and interests will remain in the land. The date for the implementation of this Act has not been announced. Trusts for sale will be abolished, as will Strict Settlements (Chapter 5). At the moment they are still extant.

The creation of a trust for sale

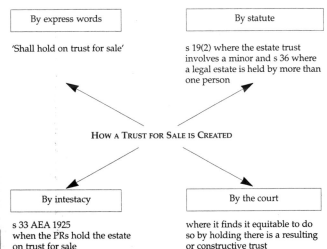

By express words

'Shall hold on trust for sale'

By statute

s 19(2) where the estate trust involves a minor and s 36 where a legal estate is held by more than one person

HOW A TRUST FOR SALE IS CREATED

By intestacy

s 33 AEA 1925 when the PRs hold the estate on trust for sale

By the court

where it finds it equitable to do so by holding there is a resulting or constructive trust

The role of the trustees in a trust for sale

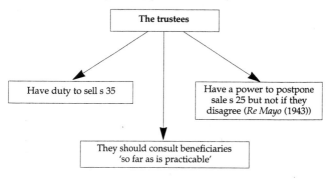

The trustees

Have duty to sell s 35

Have a power to postpone sale s 25 but not if they disagree (*Re Mayo* (1943))

They should consult beneficiaries 'so far as is practicable'

The use of s 30

This allows beneficiaries as 'persons interested' to apply to the court for an order for sale.

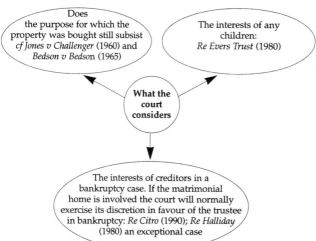

Does the purpose for which the property was bought still subsist *cf Jones v Challenger* (1960) and *Bedson v Bedson* (1965)

The interests of any children: *Re Evers Trust* (1980)

What the court considers

The interests of creditors in a bankruptcy case. If the matrimonial home is involved the court will normally exercise its discretion in favour of the trustee in bankruptcy: *Re Citro* (1990); *Re Halliday* (1980) an exceptional case

Trusts for sale: co-ownership, spouses and cohabitees

Problems arise when the legal title is held by one person only, when more than that person has an interest in a property, particularly when it is the house they inhabit.

This is because a legal interest in land is only acquired by ss 52 and 53(1) of the LPA 1925.

The courts have sought, in the case of those who have no legal title, to find an equitable interest under a resulting, implied or constructive trust so bringing them within s 53(2).

A resulting trust

X and Y buy property.
Both contribute to the purchase price

↓

Only X's name is on the conveyance
so X alone holds the legal title

↓

Y's direct contribution to the purchase price
gives him an equitable interest in the property in proportion
to his contribution under a resulting trust

↓

X holds the property on trust for a sale for himself and Y

↓

Because there is a trust for sale, any sale of the property
requires payment to two trustees (s 27 LPA 1925)

Note

1 The key word is purchase. There will be no resulting trust if there was a gift of money to make the purchase. Where there is a loan from one set of parents to buy a matrimonial home, even when only one spouse's name is on the title, the loan is deemed to be to the couple jointly, so that the other will have made a contribution: *Halifax Building Society v Brown* (1995).

2 Where the title is in one name but the equitable interest was declared to be held as joint tenants, then each has one half, regardless of individual contribution.

A constructive trust

Whereas a resulting trust depends on a *direct* contribution to the purchase price (either by initial payment or mortgage instalments) a constructive trust is related to an indirect contribution.

The landmark case of *Lloyds Bank v Rosset* (1991) reviewed the whole area of constructive trusts as applied to co-ownership and considered the factors necessary to establish the two elements of common intention and indirection contribution to the purchase of the co-ownership property.

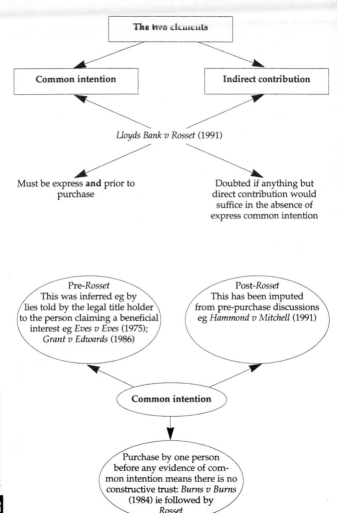

The two elements

Common intention

Indirect contribution

Lloyds Bank v Rosset (1991)

Must be express **and** prior to purchase

Doubted if anything but direct contribution would suffice in the absence of express common intention

Pre-*Rosset*
This was inferred eg by lies told by the legal title holder to the person claiming a beneficial interest eg *Eves v Eves* (1975); *Grant v Edwards* (1986)

Post-*Rosset*
This has been imputed from pre-purchase discussions eg *Hammond v Mitchell* (1991)

Common intention

Purchase by one person before any evidence of common intention means there is no constructive trust: *Burns v Burns* (1984) ie followed by *Rosset*

Where common intention established

Only where common intention is established will the second limb, indirect contribution, be considered.

It must be remembered that Lord Bridge said that, in the absence of an express common intention, he doubted whether anything less than a direct contribution to the purchase price would suffice to give a beneficial interest in the property under a constructive trust.

Indirect contribution

The person with the legal title cannot afford to pay the purchase price (usually via the mortgage) and meet his other commitments eg household bills

so

the person claiming a beneficial interest pays for some of his commitments eg goes to work to pay the household bills and clothe the children. This enables the legal title holder to pay the mortgage.

Cases illustrating indirect contribution

The earlier cases of *Gissing v Gissing* and *Pettitt v Pettitt*, both 1970, required the indirect contribution to be in money or money's worth. Bringing up the children and running the household was deemed insufficient.

But in *Grant v Edwards* (1986) contributing to the household expenses so the legal title holder could pay the mortgage was deemed sufficient.

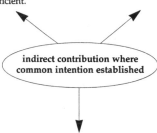

indirect contribution where common intention established

In the post-*Rosset* case of *Hammond v Mitchell* it was held that the court will examine conduct which can be attributed to action based on the established common intention.

Note: *Burns v Burns* (1984).

The facts   A couple cohabited for 19 years. They had children and the woman took his name. Then he asked her to leave.

Held   She had no interest in the property. Bringing up the children and keeping the house and buying some furniture were not acts sufficient to give her an interest in the house.

In any case her lover had bought the house before she went there to live with him and there had never been on his part an intention she should have a share in it.

Co-ownership and occupation

Co-ownership always means a trust for sale so:

The doctrine of conversion always applies, so

the interests of the co-owners are always in money, so

if the property is sold and the money paid to two trustees s 27 LPA 1925

the interests of the co-owners are over-reached; the purchaser is not required to ascertain anything else.

This means that the purchaser should be able to obtain possession of the house, but this is not always the case.

If a person who has an interest in the property under a trust for sale is in occupation of it different rules apply, according to whether the land is registered or unregistered.

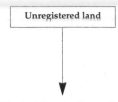

| Unregistered land |

The doctrine of notice applies:
Kingsnorth Finance v Tizzard (1986)

A person with a beneficial interest in the property he occupies does not have an overriding interest under s 70(1)(g) LRA 1925 and cannot be removed from the property (*Williams & Glyn's Bank v Boland* (1981)), even if the purchaser could not have found out about the interest, and if he could not have known the purchase money should be paid to two trustees.

BUT

In *City of London BS v Flegg* (1988) the land was registered and there were four co-owners who were trustees under the trust. When two of them mortgaged the property without the knowledge of the other two, who also occupied the property, and defaulted on the repayments, the Building Society were allowed to obtain possession. This means if the purchase money is paid to two trustees the overriding interest is negated.

Spouses and occupation

These come within two Acts as regards co-ownership:

MHA 1983	Section 37 MP AND PA 1970
This gives a spouse a right not to be evicted or excluded from the matrimonial home without a court order. The right is registrable as a Class F land charge for unregistered land and as a minor interest for registered land. It does not give a proprietary interest in land.	If a spouse makes a substantial contribution in money or money's worth to improvements to the property that spouse will be given a share in a beneficial interest in a ratio to that contribution.

5 Settlements

It should be remembered here that this whole chapter will be out of date when the Trusts of Land and Appointment of Trustees Act 1996 is brought into being although, at the date of writing, the date for the implementation of the Act has not been announced.

There are two types:

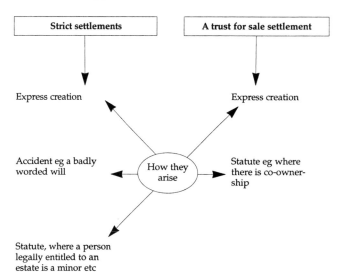

Strict settlements

Express creation by words such as, 'To X for life, then Y' (in two ways, either *inter vivos* or by will).

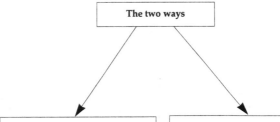

The two ways

By will: s 6 of the SLA 1926

requires:
a) the will which is deemed to be the trust instrument
b) the PRs to vest the legal estate in the tenant for life

Inter vivos: **s 4 of the SLA 1925**

requires:
a) a vesting deed transferring the estate to the tenant for life
b) a trust instrument declaring terms of the trust

The tenant for life and his powers
Who is he?

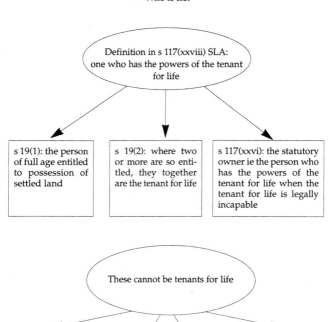

Definition in s 117(xxviii) SLA:
one who has the powers of the tenant
for life

s 19(1): the person
of full age entitled
to possession of
settled land

s 19(2): where two
or more are so enti-
tled, they together
are the tenant for life

s 117(xxvi): the statutory
owner ie the person who
has the powers of the
tenant for life when the
tenant for life is legally
incapable

These cannot be tenants for life

Anyone paying rent
even if only a nomi-
nal one:
Re Catling (1931)

Anyone paid a fixed
annuity from the
estate:
Re Jeffreys (1931)

Anyone having only part of
the income from the estate:
Re Frewn (1926)

Where the trustees are given
a discretion to pay the bene-
ficiary an income or not:
Re Gallenga (1938)

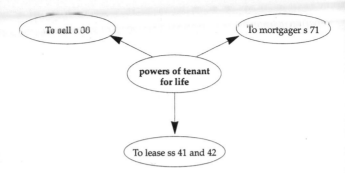

To sell s 38

To mortgager s 71

powers of tenant
for life

To lease ss 41 and 42

1) If he sells, the purchase
money must be paid to two
trustees, s 18 SLA 1925. Then
beneficial interests of others are
overreached and are in the capital sum. The tenant for life gets
the income from this sum

2) He must sell for the best price
reasonably obtainable, s 39 SLA
1925:
Wheelwright v Walker (1883)

but

**The power to sell cannot
be prevented s 104**

except

Section 65. The date and form of
the settlement may prevent sale
of the house if it is the principal
mansion house ie over 25 acres
and not a farmhouse

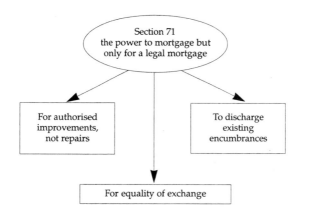

Building leases limited to 999 years   Mining leases limited to 100 years

Sections 41 and 42
power to grant leases

Forestry leases limited to 999 years   Other leases limited to 50 years

Section 71
the power to mortgage but
only for a legal mortgage

For authorised
improvements,
not repairs

To discharge
existing
encumbrances

For equality of exchange

Problems arising

Problems arise because the SLA 1925 tries to ensure secrecy of the trust in accordance with the 'curtain' principle adopted in the 1925 legislation.

Section 13: the 'paralysing section'

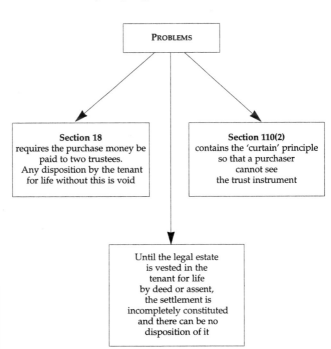

PROBLEMS

Section 18
requires the purchase money be paid to two trustees.
Any disposition by the tenant for life without this is void

Section 110(2)
contains the 'curtain' principle so that a purchaser cannot see the trust instrument

Until the legal estate is vested in the tenant for life by deed or assent, the settlement is incompletely constituted and there can be no disposition of it

Section 110(1)
makes it clear that a *purchaser*
dealing with a tenant for life
'in good faith' takes,
even if the requirements of s 18
are not met

CONFLICTING CASES

Re Morgans Lease (1970):

s 110(1) does apply to a purchaser who acted in good faith even if he did not know he was dealing with settled land

Weston v Henshaw (1950):

A person who deals with the tenant for life as absolute owner in not a *bona fide* purchaser

6 Easements and profits à prendre

Characteristics of an easement

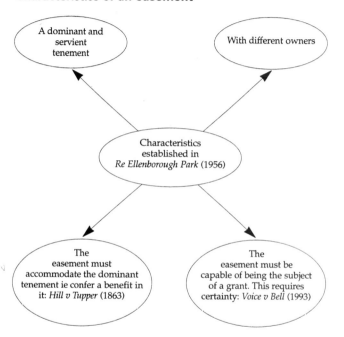

A dominant and servient tenement

With different owners

Characteristics established in *Re Ellenborough Park* (1956)

The easement must accommodate the dominant tenement ie confer a benefit in it: *Hill v Tupper* (1863)

The easement must be capable of being the subject of a grant. This requires certainty: *Voice v Bell* (1993)

Note

What is capable of being an easement is a matter of case law. As society changes new easements may be allowed.

The category 'is not closed': Lord St Leonards in *Dyce v Lady James Hay* (1852).

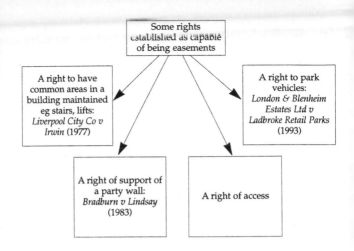

Some rights established as capable of being easements

A right to have common areas in a building maintained eg stairs, lifts: *Liverpool City Co v Irwin* (1977)

A right to park vehicles: *London & Blenheim Estates Ltd v Ladbroke Retail Parks* (1993)

A right of support of a party wall: *Bradburn v Lindsay* (1983)

A right of access

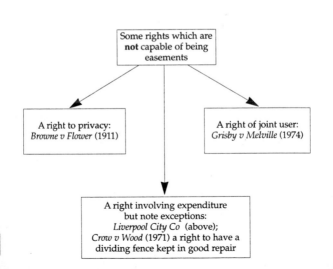

Some rights which are **not** capable of being easements

A right to privacy: *Browne v Flower* (1911)

A right of joint user: *Grisby v Melville* (1974)

A right involving expenditure but note exceptions: *Liverpool City Co* (above); *Crow v Wood* (1971) a right to have a dividing fence kept in good repair

The creation of easements

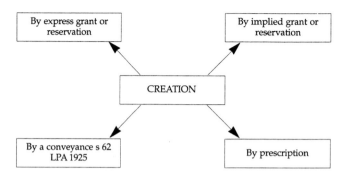

By express grant or reservation

By implied grant or reservation

CREATION

By a conveyance s 62 LPA 1925

By prescription

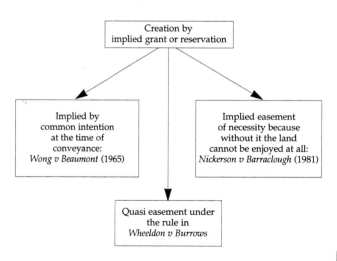

Creation by implied grant or reservation

Implied by common intention at the time of conveyance: *Wong v Beaumont* (1965)

Implied easement of necessity because without it the land cannot be enjoyed at all: *Nickerson v Barraclough* (1981)

Quasi easement under the rule in *Wheeldon v Burrows*

The rule in *Wheeldon v Burrows*

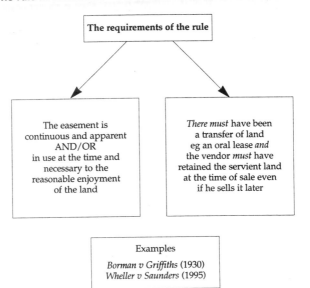

The requirements of the rule

The easement is
continuous and apparent
AND/OR
in use at the time and
necessary to the
reasonable enjoyment
of the land

There must have been
a transfer of land
eg an oral lease *and*
the vendor *must* have
retained the servient land
at the time of sale even
if he sells it later

Examples

Borman v Griffiths (1930)
Wheller v Saunders (1995)

Creation by s 62 LPA 1925

Section 62 implies into all conveyances made by deed, that
privileges existing at the time of the conveyance become
rights.

Wright v Macadam (1949) is the authority.

Creation by prescription

There are three forms of prescription:

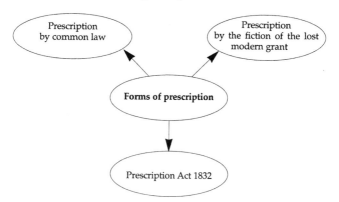

Note

All forms of prescription require the following:

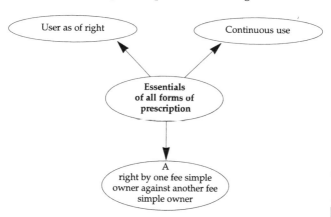

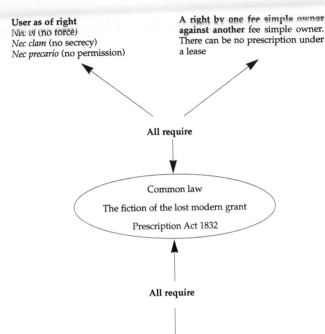

User as of right
Nec vi (no force)
Nec clam (no secrecy)
Nec precario (no permission)

A right by one fee simple owner against another fee simple owner. There can be no prescription under a lease

All require

Common law

The fiction of the lost modern grant

Prescription Act 1832

All require

Continuous use
This does not mean it cannot be interrupted.
Toleration of use is deemed consent:
Mills v Silver (1991)

Prescription by common law requires long user

This means from *time immemorial*, ie 1189, but proof of the right has existed
for 20 years suffices unless it can be rebutted
by showing:

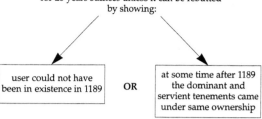

| user could not have been in existence in 1189 | **OR** | at some time after 1189 the dominant and servient tenements came under same ownership |

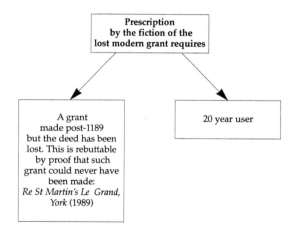

| **Prescription by the fiction of the lost modern grant requires** |

| A grant made post-1189 but the deed has been lost. This is rebuttable by proof that such grant could never have been made: *Re St Martin's Le Grand, York* (1989) | 20 year user |

The Prescription Act 1832

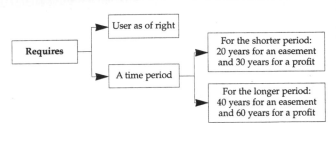

Requires
- User as of right
- A time period
  - For the shorter period: 20 years for an easement and 30 years for a profit
  - For the longer period: 40 years for an easement and 60 years for a profit

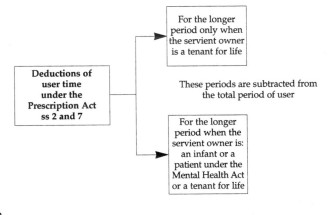

Deductions of user time under the Prescription Act ss 2 and 7
- For the longer period only when the servient owner is a tenant for life
- For the longer period when the servient owner is: an infant or a patient under the Mental Health Act or a tenant for life

These periods are subtracted from the total period of user

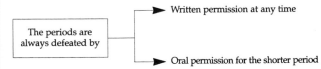

The periods are always defeated by
- Written permission at any time
- Oral permission for the shorter period

Easement of light: s 3 of the Prescription Act 1832

Section 3 requires
- 20 years enjoyment of light
- No user as of right provided there is no written agreement
- No fee simple owner requirements, a tenant can acquire the right against his landlord

Note

The Right to Light Act 1959 allows a servient owner to register a notice as a local land charge so that if the dominant owner does not object within one year there will be deemed an interruption to the right to light.

The test for light is: how much is there *not* how much is lost.

In *Collis v Home & Colonial Stores* (1904) the test was held to be: is there sufficient for the beneficial use of business premises and for comfort in a dwelling house?

Greenhouses: *Allen v Greenwood* (1979) established a new easement of light to a greenhouse which must be sufficient for the growth of plants.

Legal easements

These are created by deed, statute or prescription

Unregistered land

a right *in rem* is good against the whole world 1925

Registered land

an overriding interest under s 70(1)(a) LRA

Equitable easements

Unregistered land

Class D(ii) land charge if created post-1925, *Shiloh Spinners v Harding* (1973) otherwise the doctrine of notice

Registered land

Problem: *Celsteel v Alton House Holdings* (1985)

7 Leases

Definition

Section 205(xxvii) LPA (1925): 'a term of years' and this includes fractions of a year and a term of less than one year.

Requirements

There are four:

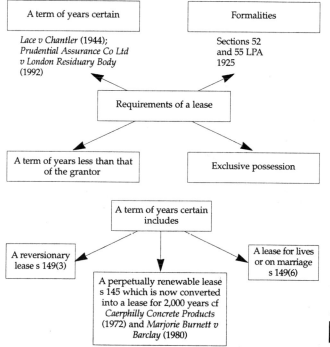

Formalities for a legal lease

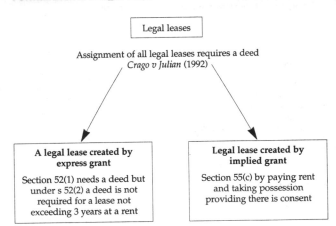

Legal leases

Assignment of all legal leases requires a deed
Crago v Julian (1992)

A legal lease created by express grant	Legal lease created by implied grant
Section 52(1) needs a deed but under s 52(2) a deed is not required for a lease not exceeding 3 years at a rent	Section 55(c) by paying rent and taking possession providing there is consent

Exclusive possession

Unless there is exclusive possession there cannot be a lease, but exclusive possession does not mean there is always a lease. A lease gives protection under the Rent Act 1977 and the Housing Act 1988 for tenants of dwelling houses. If there is no lease, there is only a licence which does not come within these Acts.

Key case: *Street v Mountford* (1985).

Lord Templeman said that what an agreement was called did not matter; if there was exclusive possession at a rent it was a lease.

An occupier can only be a lodger (a licence) or a lessee (lease).

Cases following *Street v Mountford* where the courts have differentiated between a lease and a licence

Decided the same day by the House of Lords in 1990

A-G Securities v Vaughan	*Antoniades v Villiers*
Four people sharing a four bed-roomed flat. Had identical agreements termed licences. Each was for six months without the right to exclusive possession of any part of the flat. It included provision for a new person to replace one who left, to be mutually agreed.	Cohabitees shared a flat. Each had an agreement entitled a licence, stating that the landlord could use the room at the same time and allow others to do so.
Held: They only had licences. There was no joint tenancy which could amount to a lease. Their agreements were between the landlord and individuals.	**Held:** They had a lease. They were living in one room and sharing a bed; no one could ever have believed the landlord would share it. The agreement was a sham.

See also *Aslan v Murphy* (1989); *Skipton Building Society v Clayton* (1993).

Instances where although there is exclusive possession, there can be no lease

Although there cannot be a lease without exclusive possession, it is possible to have exclusive possession, yet not have a lease.

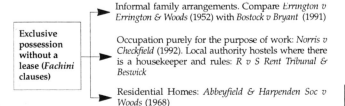

Exclusive possession without a lease (*Fachini* clauses)	Informal family arrangements. Compare *Errington v Errington & Woods* (1952) with *Bostock v Bryant* (1991)
	Occupation purely for the purpose of work: *Norris v Checkfield* (1992). Local authority hostels where there is a housekeeper and rules: *R v S Rent Tribunal & Beswick*
	Residential Homes: *Abbeyfield & Harpenden Soc v Woods* (1968)

Types and determination of tenancies

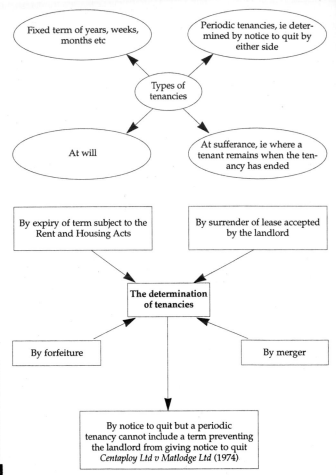

Breaches of covenant

When a tenant commits a breach of covenant, the landlord may choose one of the following remedies:

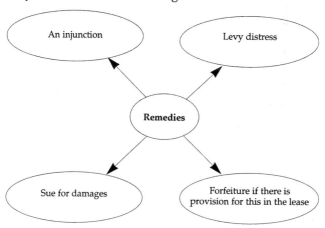

Forfeiture

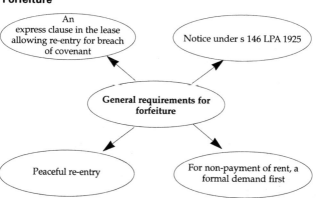

Particular requirements

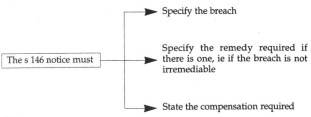

The s 146 notice must
→ Specify the breach
→ Specify the remedy required if there is one, ie if the breach is not irremediable
→ State the compensation required

Note

The landlord must not have waived his right to forfeiture by his acts, eg by accepting rent during or after the breach: *Central Estates Ltd v Woolgas* (1972).

Some breaches are regarded as incapable of remedy, ie are irremediable breaches, but circumstances may allow a modification of the case.

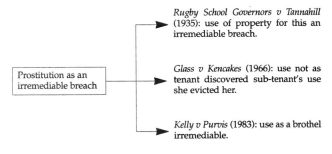

Prostitution as an irremediable breach
→ *Rugby School Governors v Tannahill* (1935): use of property for this an irremediable breach.
→ *Glass v Kencakes* (1966): use not as tenant discovered sub-tenant's use she evicted her.
→ *Kelly v Purvis* (1983): use as a brothel irremediable.

The test seems to be: can the breach actually be remedied? The key case is *Expert Clothing Service and Sales Ltd v Hillgate Home Ltd* (1986). If the damage caused by the breach cannot be rectified, then the breach is irremediable.

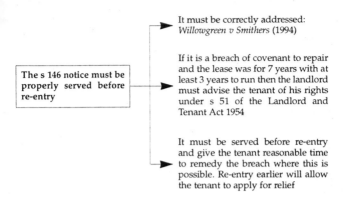

The s 146 notice must be properly served before re-entry	It must be correctly addressed: *Willowgreen v Smithers* (1994)
	If it is a breach of covenant to repair and the lease was for 7 years with at least 3 years to run then the landlord must advise the tenant of his rights under s 51 of the Landlord and Tenant Act 1954
	It must be served before re-entry and give the tenant reasonable time to remedy the breach where this is possible. Re-entry earlier will allow the tenant to apply for relief

A tenant may serve a counter-notice on the landlord within 28 days requiring him to obtain a court order for possession.

If the landlord brings an action for possession, the tenant can apply for relief under s 146(2) and the court will exercise its discretion in the matter.

This applies even if the landlord has re-entered and sold the property in the meantime: *Bhojwani v Kingsley Ltd* (1992).

Forfeiture for non-payment of rent
This differs from the normal procedure for forfeiture.

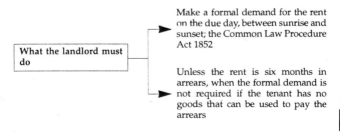

| What the landlord must do | Make a formal demand for the rent on the due day, between sunrise and sunset; the Common Law Procedure Act 1852 |
| | Unless the rent is six months in arrears, when the formal demand is not required if the tenant has no goods that can be used to pay the arrears |

The Law Commission Report 1994 on the determination of tenancies

The 1994 Report has been followed by a draft bill but as yet no Act. The Commission recommended:

No forfeiture for breach of covenant by a tenant.

No need for a clause in the tenancy agreement giving a right of re-entry for a landlord to be able to bring proceedings for termination of the tenancy.

The Law Commission's recommendations 1994

The landlord can only bring proceedings if he can show a breach of covenant or inability to pay rent because of insolvency.

A successful plea by the landlord should mean: either an absolute termination of the tenancy or a remedial order so that there will be termination only if the breach is not satisfactorily remedied.

The assignment of leases

A leaseholder who has a long lease may find that his circumstances have changed and he no longer requires that land. He may then decide to sell the remaining years of his lease to another. This is an assignment.

To be legal the assignment must be by deed: *Crago v Julian* (1992).

Section 19(1) Landlord and Tenant Act 1927	Even if a lease has an express clause against assignment, the landlord shall not refuse consent except on reasonable grounds.
Landlord and Tenant Act 1988	Requires a landlord to consider a written request by a tenant to assign his lease, and give either consent (specifying any restrictions) or refuse consent giving reasons. (Such refusal cannot be based on personal characteristics such as the colour of hair.)

Air India v Balabel (1993)

The lease
A 20 year lease contained a clause against assignment without the landlord's consent and that such consent should not be unreasonably withheld.

The facts
The tenant applied for consent and the landlord refused giving written reasons. The tenant still assigned the lease.

The landlord began proceedings for forfeiture.

Held: The landlord could do so. The proposed tenants to whom the lease was assigned had a record of not paying rent and proposed to run a business on the premises which had already failed elsewhere. The landlord was entitled to consider such matters.

Leasehold covenants: enforceability

This has been modified by the Landlord and Tenant (Covenants) Act 1995 which affects all covenants made after 1 January 1996.

The main differences are that it removes the necessity for a leasehold covenant to 'have reference to the subject matter of the lease,' and removes privity of contract between original landlord and original tenant.

A covenant is a promise made by deed.

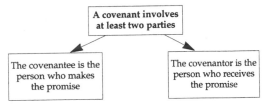

Burdens and benefits

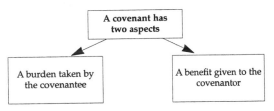

The parties who make the covenant are the original parties but both the covenantee and the covenantor may cease to own or lease the land which is subject to the covenant. Whether or not the covenant is still enforceable by the person holding the benefited land depends on the various conveyances and the time at which they were made.

The following situations are possible:

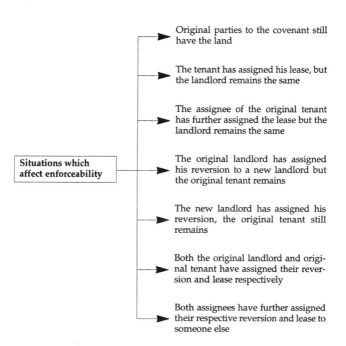

Situations which affect enforceability	→	Original parties to the covenant still have the land
	→	The tenant has assigned his lease, but the landlord remains the same
	→	The assignee of the original tenant has further assigned the lease but the landlord remains the same
	→	The original landlord has assigned his reversion to a new landlord but the original tenant remains
	→	The new landlord has assigned his reversion, the original tenant still remains
	→	Both the original landlord and original tenant have assigned their reversion and lease respectively
	→	Both assignees have further assigned their respective reversion and lease to someone else

Note

Once the original landlord has assigned his reversion he can only sue the original tenant for damages not for specific performance.

The position of the original parties to the covenant
This has now changed.

The position for covenants made before 1 January 1996
There is privity of contract between the original parties to
the covenant so that they are always liable for any breach
they may commit.

This applies whatever the nature of the covenant and
whether or not they have continued to own or lease the land
to which the covenant applies.

Landlord L

Land leased to X who
covenants to refrain
from keeping pigs on it

X assigns his lease to Y
who then keeps pigs
on it

Result:
The original landlord L can sue the original tenant X for
breach of covenant even though X has not carried out the breach:
Herbert Duncan Ltd v Cluttons (1992)

*The position for leasehold covenants made after 31
December 1995*
These are subject to s 5(1) of the new Landlord and Tenant
(Covenants) Act 1995.

Landlords of leases created after that date will not be able to sue ex-tenants for breach of covenant on the basis of privity of contract.

This means the original tenant will no longer be liable on the whole term of the lease, unless this is an express term of the lease.

Enforceability of leasehold covenants when the tenant has assigned his lease

For leases made before 1 January 1996
There is always privity of estate between a landlord and a person who is not the original tenant but someone to whom that tenant has assigned his lease.

If the covenant is to be enforceable against the assignee of the lease, certain conditions must be fulfilled:

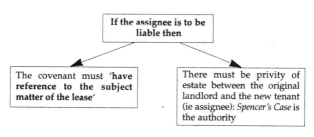

Meaning of having reference to the subject matter of the lease

This was set out as a three-pronged test in:

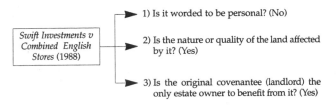

Swift Investments v Combined English Stores (1988)

1) Is it worded to be personal? (No)

2) Is the nature or quality of the land affected by it? (Yes)

3) Is the original covenantee (landlord) the only estate owner to benefit from it? (Yes)

For leases made after 31 December 1995

The new Act abolishes the requirement that the covenant should 'have reference to the subject matter of the lease.

This means that covenants will be deemed to have passed the burden to the assignee unless they are *expressed* to be personal.

Enforceability of leasehold covenants when there has been more than one assignment of the lease

For leases made before 1 January 1996

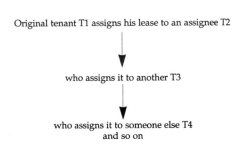

Original tenant T1 assigns his lease to an assignee T2

who assigns it to another T3

who assigns it to someone else T4
and so on

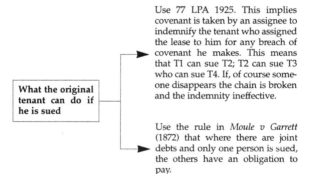

What can T1 do if he is sued?

For leases made after 31 December 1995

The new Act releases all assignees of the original tenant from any future liabilities for breach of covenant when they assign the lease. This means the landlord can only sue the present tenant ie T4.

Enforceability of leasehold covenants when the original landlord has assigned his reversion

In this situation the landlord changes and the tenant remains the same. Can the new landlord sue his new tenant for breach of covenant and vice versa?

Yes

because of ss 141 and 142 LPA 1925 provided the covenant has reference to the subject matter of the lease.

Note

Once the original landlord assigns his reversion he loses the right to sue the original tenant although the original tenant can still sue the original landlord.

The position for leases made after 31 December 1995 under the Landlord and Tenant (Covenants) Act 1995

There is no longer privity of contract between the original parties so they can no longer sue, but the same position exists between the new landlord and tenant as above with the difference that the covenant no longer has to have 'reference to the subject matter of the lease'.

Enforceability of leasehold covenants when there has been more than one assignment of the reversion by successive landlords

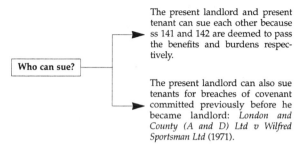

Who can sue?

The present landlord and present tenant can sue each other because ss 141 and 142 are deemed to pass the benefits and burdens respectively.

The present landlord can also sue tenants for breaches of covenant committed previously before he became landlord: *London and County (A and D) Ltd v Wilfred Sportsman Ltd* (1971).

Leasehold covenants and sub-tenants

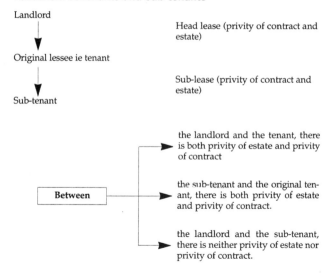

Landlord

Head lease (privity of contract and estate)

Original lessee ie tenant

Sub-lease (privity of contract and estate)

Sub-tenant

Between

the landlord and the tenant, there is both privity of estate and privity of contract

the sub-tenant and the original tenant, there is both privity of estate and privity of contract.

the landlord and the sub-tenant, there is neither privity of estate nor privity of contract.

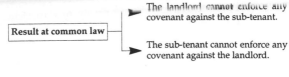

| Result at common law | The landlord cannot enforce any covenant against the sub-tenant. |
| | The sub-tenant cannot enforce any covenant against the landlord. |

BUT

If the sub-tenant breaches a covenant the tenant is still liable to the landlord. The landlord may then demand forfeiture if there is a relevant clause in the lease. This means the sub-tenant's lease is also determined.

The landlord may be able to proceed directly against a sub-tenant who has broken a covenant in equity under the rule in *Tulk v Moxhay* (1848).

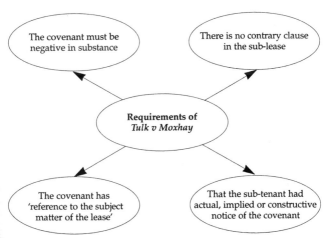

The covenant must be negative in substance

There is no contrary clause in the sub-lease

Requirements of *Tulk v Moxhay*

The covenant has 'reference to the subject matter of the lease'

That the sub-tenant had actual, implied or constructive notice of the covenant

Under this rule, the sub-tenant's lease will not become forfeit but the landlord may be awarded damages or granted an injunction to prevent further breaches.

Where a sub-tenant finds his lessor's lease (ie the tenant's lease) has become forfeit so that his lease is also determined he can apply to the court for relief under s 146 LPA 1925.

Implied covenants

What are called 'usual' covenants are implied into leases by law.

The most important is that the landlord will allow his tenant 'quiet enjoyment' ie that he will be free from any harassment. Any harassment by, or on behalf of the landlord is a criminal offence under the Protection from Eviction Act 1977.

The Leasehold Reform Act 1967

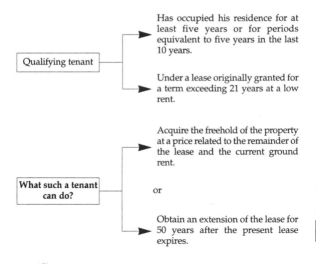

Qualifying tenant
→ Has occupied his residence for at least five years or for periods equivalent to five years in the last 10 years.
→ Under a lease originally granted for a term exceeding 21 years at a low rent.

What such a tenant can do?
→ Acquire the freehold of the property at a price related to the remainder of the lease and the current ground rent.

or

→ Obtain an extension of the lease for 50 years after the present lease expires.

The Leasehold Reform Housing and Urban Development Act 1993

This gives new rights to those living in flats, including:

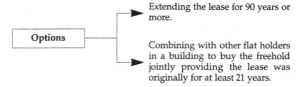

Options

Extending the lease for 90 years or more.

Combining with other flat holders in a building to buy the freehold jointly providing the lease was originally for at least 21 years.

8 Licences

A licence means that an owner of land has given another person or persons the right to go on to or to use his land. Unlike a lease, there are no formalities required for a licence, mere permission from the owner is sufficient. No proprietary right is given, though the courts have sometimes actually appeared to do this.

There are four types of licences depending on the nature of the permission.

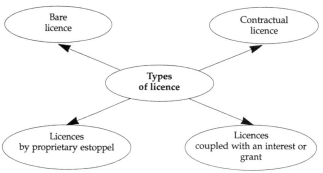

A **bare** licence	This is mere permission, allowing acts granted by the permission only. If permission is withdrawn the person becomes a trespasser. It is a purely personal right given to the licensee.
A **licence** coupled with a grant or interest	This is permission given so that a person who has a profit à prendre or some other similar right which requires going on to land belonging to someone else may enter on to such land.

Contractual licences and **licences by estoppel are more** significant because the courts have sometimes found them to give rights in the nature of proprietary rights without the need for the formalities of s 52 and s 53(1) of the LPA 1925. In such cases equity has intervened.

Contractual licences

The requirements of a contractual licence are those of contract law:

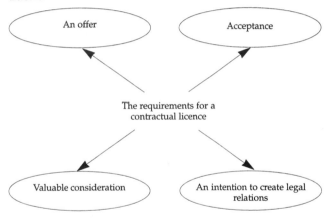

Problem

Informal family agreements

Was there an intention to create a legal relationship? The problem was discussed in *Errington v Errington and Woods* (1956). Sometimes the courts will impute such intention from the circumstances of the case as they did in *Errington*

The case: *Errington v Errington and Woods* (1956)

The facts:

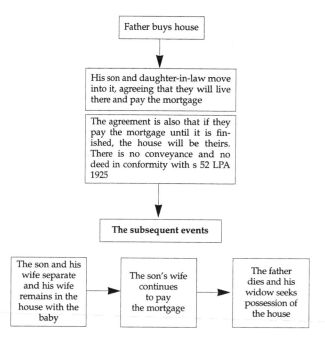

Lord Denning decided that in this case there was an intention to create legal relations and since the mortgage payments were valuable consideration, there was a contractual licence.

The following cases illustrate the nature of a contractual licence. They all concern mistresses.

Tanner v Tanner (1963)

A mistress and her children went to live in a house bought for them by her lover. He claimed possession when they quarrelled

Horrocks v Foray (1976)

A lover installed his mistress and her child in a house he owned. When he died his wife claimed possession of the house

The common facts

Coombes v Smith (1986)

A married woman left her husband to live with her lover by whom she had a child. He evicted her when they quarrelled

Tanner v Tanner

She had left a protected tenancy to live with him. This was valuable consideration and an intention to create a legal relationship. There *was* a contractual licence.

Horrocks v Foray

There was no valuable consideration, nor an intention to create a legal relationship, so there was *no* contractual licence

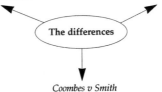

The differences

Coombes v Smith

She had provided no valuable consideration and there was no intention to create legal relations

Can a contractual licence be revoked ?

The position is different as between common law and equity.

At common law

Answer: **Yes**

Common law treats a contractual licence as subject to contract law, so that the remedy for revocation is to sue for breach of contract. Once the licence is revoked the former licensee becomes a trespasser.

In equity

Answer : **It depends**

The court will construe the agreement to discover whether or not it would be inequitable to allow revocation or not.

The following cases illustrate this:

Winter Garden Theatre (London) Ltd
v Millenium Productions Ltd (1948)

The House of Lords held that whether a contractual licence was revocable or not depended on the terms of the agreement

Hounslow LBC v Twickenham
Garden Developments (1971)

The court refused to grant an injunction to prevent the Ps from entering a site to fulfil their contract. It was irrelevant that the licence to enter was not the main purpose of the contract

BUT

Where the licence is the only agreement and sole interest, the court will grant specific performance

Verral v Great Yarmouth (1981)

Note

In *Tanner* the contractual licence was held to be irrevocable until her children had left school. Courts exercise discretion as regard revocation where informal agreements have been made, eg *Chandler v Kerley* (1978).

The facts:

Mr and Mrs K and their children live in house on which Mr K pays the mortgage instalments

↓

Mr K leaves after a quarrel but still pays the instalments

↓

Mrs K meets Mr C and they become lovers

↓

Mr K can no longer pay mortgage

↓

Mr and Mrs K agree to sell the house

↓

They cannot find a buyer so Mr C agrees to buy it

↓

He does so at a greatly reduced price on the understanding Mrs K and the children will live there with him

↓

Mrs K and Mr C quarrel and Mr C gives Mrs K notice to quit

↓

What has Mrs K got? A contractual licence? If so, is it revocable?

Held: It was clear Mr C had not bought the house with any intention of evicting Mrs K later, so that Mrs K did not have a contractual licence, since the house had been reduced in price because she was going to live there. The agreement between Mrs K and Mr C was meant to be binding but it could not be inferred that Mr C had intended to look after Mr Ks children for ever. The relationship between Mr C and Mrs K had ended, so the contractual licence could also be ended by reasonable notice. 12 months was reasonable notice.

Contractual licences and third parties

The question of whether a contractual licence can bind a third party, even though it is not strictly an interest in land has been the subject of much debate and changes of view over time. There have been three views.

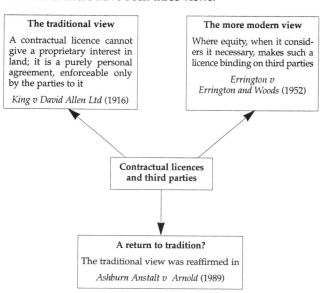

The traditional view

A contractual licence cannot give a proprietary interest in land; it is a purely personal agreement, enforceable only by the parties to it

King v David Allen Ltd (1916)

The more modern view

Where equity, when it considers it necessary, makes such a licence binding on third parties

Errington v Errington and Woods (1952)

Contractual licences and third parties

A return to tradition?

The traditional view was reaffirmed in

Ashburn Anstalt v Arnold (1989)

The more modern view owes much to Lord Denning. In *Errington v Errington and Woods*, the facts of which are given on pp 74–75, he said that it would be inequitable to allow a licence to be revoked so that a third party suffered.

He followed this some years later with his dissenting judgment in *Binions v Evans* (1972).

The facts

Husband and wife live in a cottage belonging to the estate where he works

The husband dies. His widow is allowed to stay in the cottage for life provided she keeps it tidy

Sometime later the trustees of the estate decide to sell the cottage. They inform the purchaser of the widow's occupation and, because the terms of the agreement with her are an express condition of sale, allow the purchase to be at a price below market value.

Later the purchaser tries to evict the widow from the cottage.

Lord Denning said that he could not do so. The widow, he argued had a contractual licence which could not be revoked. The purchaser had become subject to a constructive trust which prevented such eviction He had had notice of her agreement.

The majority did not agree with Lord Denning, arguing that Mrs Evans did not have a revocable tenancy-at-will but an equitable life interest under s 20(1)(iv) of the SLA 1925, ie under a strict settlement.

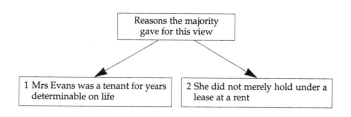

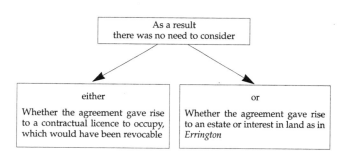

Cases such as this where occupation has been protected under a constructive trust arising from a contractual licence mean that some form of proprietary interest has been acquired without a deed or the formalities of ss 52 and 53 of the LPA 1925. The courts have sometimes limited this to a defined period of time as in *Tanner v Tanner* and *Chandler v Kerley*.

In others they appear to have created settled land without considering that as a tenant for life the occupier can sell as in the majority verdict in *Binions v Evans* considered above and in *Ungarian v Lesnoff* (1989), dealt with below.

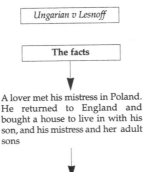

| *Ungarian v Lesnoff* |

| **The facts** |

A lover met his mistress in Poland. He returned to England and bought a house to live in with his son, and his mistress and her adult sons

He put the legal title of the house in his name only.

The mistress and her sons made many improvements to the house

When they quarrelled he sought to evict her

Did she have any interest in the house?

Held: An intention that she could live there for the rest of her life was inferred. A constructive trust resulted so that her lover held the house on trust for her. In effect this creates settled land within the SLA 1925.

A constructive trust was also found in *Re Sharpe (a Bankrupt)* (1980).

An aunt lent her nephew money to buy property

on condition she lived in it with him and was looked after

the nephew went bankrupt and the trustee in bankruptcy sought possession of the property

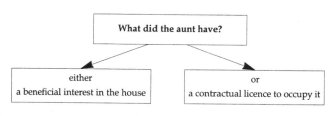

| What did the aunt have? |

either
a beneficial interest in the house

or
a contractual licence to occupy it

Held: She had a contractual licence which was not revocable until the loan was repaid. It arose under a constructive trust so her interest was binding on the trustee or any third party.

The return to tradition?

The interpretation of a contractual licence as giving rise to a constructive trust and tantamount to giving a proprietary interest in land is not always true.

In *Ashburn Anstalt v Arnold* (1989) the question of contractual licences was fully considered. Fox LJ expressed the view that it was correct that there were some instances when such a licence could give rise to a constructive trust which would make the licence binding on a third party and listed the requirements:

That it would be inequitable if the licence was not allowed to give rise to a constructive trust

because

of something the third party did, eg paid less than the market value of the property because of the licence cf *Binions*

but

this would not be a real proprietary interest in the land

because

it would be a constructive trust personally binding on that third party; it would not be binding on the land

Licences protected by estoppel

These are licences which give rise to a proprietary interest in land without the necessity of having to satisfy the formal requirements of s 52 or s 53(1) of the LPA 1925.

In these licences there can be no constructive trust because there was never any common intention between the parties that the licensee should have an interest in the land. This is so even though the licensee may have mistakenly thought there was.

Sometimes, however, it seems cases could have been decided on either basis, contractual licence or proprietary estoppel.

The requirements of proprietary estoppel

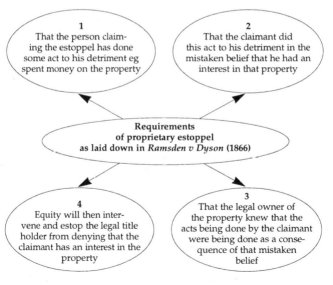

1
That the person claiming the estoppel has done some act to his detriment eg spent money on the property

2
That the claimant did this act to his detriment in the mistaken belief that he had an interest in that property

Requirements of proprietary estoppel as laid down in *Ramsden v Dyson* (1866)

4
Equity will then intervene and estop the legal title holder from denying that the claimant has an interest in the property

3
That the legal owner of the property knew that the acts being done by the claimant were being done as a consequence of that mistaken belief

Although the general requirements were affirmed in *Taylor Fashions Ltd v Liverpool Victoria Trustee Co Ltd* (1981), it was stressed in that case that the courts would adopt a less rigorous approach and that the emphasis would be on the claimant to prove that the legal owner knew he had such mistaken belief. His knowledge could be actual, implied or constructive.

In the more recent case of *Matharu v Matharu* (1994) Lord Justice Roch re-emphasised the requirements of estoppel as:

The person relying on the doctrine
has made a mistake as to his legal rights

↓

He has expended money or done
some act on the faith of that mistaken belief

↓

The possessor of the legal title knew of
his legal right and that it was inconsistent with equity

↓

The possessor of the legal right
knew of the other's mistaken belief

↓

The possessor of the legal right had encouraged
the other in the expenditure of money or doing other acts on
which that person relied for estoppel

↓

Having found the existence of proprietary
estoppel the extent of the equity must then be determined

Proprietary estoppel: what does it give the claimant?

Cases make it clear that this depends on the particular circumstances

Dillwyn v Llewellyn (1862)

A father gave his son land but only signed a memorandum. He did not convey it to him by deed as required by s 52 LPA 1925. The son built a house on the land. When his father died the land was claimed as part of his estate

Held: The executors were estopped from denying the imperfect gift. Equity demanded that the land be vested in the son

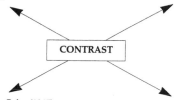

CONTRAST

Inwards v Baker (1965)

A son built a bungalow on his father's land at his father's suggestion. The son did the actual building but his father paid half the cost. The son then lived in the bungalow and believed he could do so for the rest of his life. When his father died the son discovered that the land and the bungalow had been left to another

Held: The son had acted to his detriment in the mistaken belief he could always live in the bungalow and his father had known this. The son was entitled to live there as long as he wished, if need be for life but the land would not be vested in the son

Comment

In both the cases the claimants received a proprietary interest in land without the formalities required by the LPA 1925. They did not, however receive the same rights. In *Dillwyn* the estate was vested in the son so that he became the legal title holder. In *Inwards* the son only obtained an interest which could not exceed his lifetime. What he got was more akin to a licence to use the bungalow for life.

A similar contrast exists between the following two cases

Pascoe v Turner **(1979)**

He assured his mistress that the house and its contents were hers alone

A lover bought a house for himself and his mistress to live in. The title was in his name only

Acting on this assurance she spent her own money on repairs and improvements and bought furniture

The relationship broke down and he gave his mistress notice to quit

What was she?

A volunteer certainly and 'equity will not assist a volunteer'.

Held: She was a licensee but she had acted in reliance on his promise, so he was estopped from evicting her: she had acted to her detriment on that reliance.

What is more the court not only allowed her to remain in occupation of the house, it ordered the *legal* estate to be conveyed to her so that the imperfect gift was perfected in equity.

Compare *Greasely v Cooke* (1980).

The facts:

> A widower owned the house in which he lived with his sons and mentally retarded daughter

↓

> He employs a servant to look after the daughter and run the house. One of the sons makes the servant his mistress. The servant is never paid any money but does not worry because she is told she can always live there with them

↓

> When the widower dies the sons try to evict the servant

Held: They could not do so. They were estopped. The servant had acted to her detriment in working for nothing in reliance on the promise she could always live there. The onus was on the sons as the legal title holders to rebut this and they could not do so.

Griffiths v Williams (1977) illustrates a different way the courts have used estoppel. It concerns an informal family arrangement.

> The relationships

Mrs Cole, Mrs Griffiths, her daughter Mrs Williams, Mrs G's daughter and Mrs C's granddaughter	the owner of a house who lives in the house

Mrs C tells Mrs W that
she has left her the house in her will

↓

so Mrs W spends money improving it

↓

Mrs C knows Mrs W is doing
this because she believes the house will be hers

↓

Mrs C dies having made a
new will leaving the house to Mrs G

Held: Mrs G was estopped from taking the house. Mrs W was given a lease at a nominal rent but not a life interest because that would create settled land and she could then sell.

It is clear that proprietary estoppel can be used to acquire an interest for a given period and sometimes an interest in the land itself so that it can bind a purchaser for all time.

Crab v Arun DC (1976) illustrates this.

Initial situation: both plots owned by D

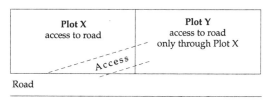

| Plot X access to road | Plot Y access to road only through Plot X |

Road

Situation after sale

| Plot X bought without reservation of access to Plot Y | Plot Y bought with oral assurance that access would be granted |

The new owner of Plot Y refuses access
The court estops D from reneging on his word
The owner of Plot Y has acquired an easement of access, ie a right
attached to the land itself

Problem: When does a licence by estoppel become an easement?

In *Arun* the position was clear but there is still much discussion in the case of *ER Ives Investments Ltd v High* (1967) where an equitable interest in the nature of an equitable easement was created but deemed to be non-registrable, so that a purchaser would not necessarily know of its existence but would still be bound by it.

The facts of the case:

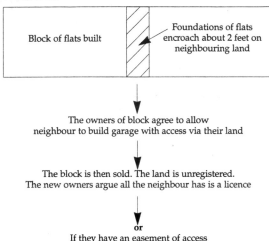

Block of flats built

Foundations of flats encroach about 2 feet on neighbouring land

The owners of block agree to allow neighbour to build garage with access via their land

The block is then sold. The land is unregistered. The new owners argue all the neighbour has is a licence

or

If they have an easement of access it is not binding on them because it has not been registered as a Class D(iii) land charge under LCA 1972

Held: The access could be seen so it was an equitable easement binding on the flats

Note

In any case the foundations had imposed a burden on the neighbouring land so that under the doctrine of mutual benefit and burden (*Halsall v Brizzel* (1957)) the benefit of the access would have been allowed.

Further problem

If the land had been registered would the easement have become an overriding interest within s 70(1)(a) of the LRA 1925?

There is still doubt as to whether this is really an equitable easement or a licence by estoppel. If it is an easement, the problem of registration both for registered and unregistered land is still not resolved.

The problem of *Re Basham* (1986)

Mother remarries and takes her 16 year old daughter to live with her in her husband's house. She helps in the house and in her stepfather's business

When her mother dies she continues to do this but moves away when she marries. She and her husband and son move back to the area to be near her stepfather when he is ill, to help him

She arranges for central heating in his house, cooks and looks after him and her husband does the garden but they live in their own house. The old man repeatedly promised to leave her the house and says her son will be looked after

Her stepfather dies intestate

The solicitors ask the court's advice

Held: The **entire** estate should go to the stepdaughter. She gained it by estoppel

Problem:
How can estoppel be exercised in the future? After he is dead?

Academics have surmised that this decision was due to:

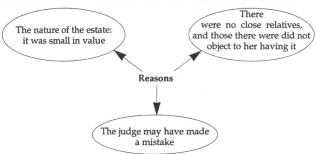

Re Basham also raises the question of what would have happened if the stepfather had left a will or bequeathed the cottage to someone else, or been living in it as a tenant having sold it some time before.

Similar problems centred on informal promises were raised again in *Lim Teng Huan v Ang Swee Chan* (1992), where a written agreement (not a deed) was held to be unenforceable but was made, in effect, enforceable by proprietary estoppel.

9 Freehold covenants

Definition

A covenant is a promise made by deed. The person making the promise is the covenantor; the person who takes the promise is the *covenantee*.

A restrictive covenant is made between holders of freehold land ie owners of a fee simple absolute in possession.

Covenants may be positive or negative.

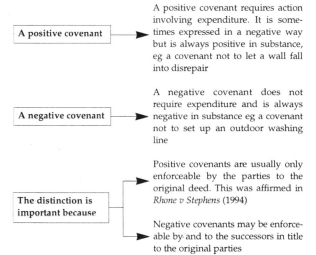

A positive covenant ➤ A positive covenant requires action involving expenditure. It is sometimes expressed in a negative way but is always positive in substance, eg a covenant not to let a wall fall into disrepair

A negative covenant ➤ A negative covenant does not require expenditure and is always negative in substance eg a covenant not to set up an outdoor washing line

The distinction is important because ➤ Positive covenants are usually only enforceable by the parties to the original deed. This was affirmed in *Rhone v Stephens* (1994)

➤ Negative covenants may be enforceable by and to the successors in title to the original parties

What happens if the original parties sell their land?

The original parties to the covenant are always liable on it. What happens when one or both parties sell their land must always be considered at both common law and in equity and in terms of the benefit and the burden.

The burdens of restrictive covenants

What happens when the burdened land has been sold to someone else?

At common law

The burden of a covenant, positive or negative, will not run at common law on the authority of *Austerberry v Oldham Corporation* (1885), so that a covenantee cannot enforce the burden of a covenant against the successor-in-title of the original covenantor.

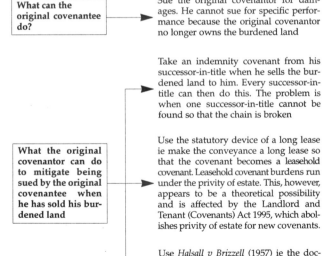

What can the original covenantee do?

Sue the original covenantor for damages. He cannot sue for specific performance because the original covenantor no longer owns the burdened land

What the original covenantor can do to mitigate being sued by the original covenantee when he has sold his burdened land

Take an indemnity covenant from his successor-in-title when he sells the burdened land to him. Every successor-in-title can then do this. The problem is when one successor-in-title cannot be found so that the chain is broken

Use the statutory device of a long lease ie make the conveyance a long lease so that the covenant becomes a leasehold covenant. Leasehold covenant burdens run under the privity of estate. This, however, appears to be a theoretical possibility and is affected by the Landlord and Tenant (Covenants) Act 1995, which abolishes privity of estate for new covenants.

Use *Halsall v Brizzell* (1957) ie the doctrine of mutual benefit and burden, so that if the burdened land also enjoys a benefit, it must accept the burden

Note

It has been argued that, since s 78 of the LPA 1925 was held to pass the benefit of a covenant in *Federated Homes v Mill Lodge Properties Ltd* (1981), then s 79 should serve to pass the benefit. This would negate *Austerberry v Oldham Corporation*.

It should be remembered, however, that before *Federated Homes*, Lord Upjohn said in *Topham Ltd v Earl of Sefton* (1966) that s 79 did not mean that the burden of a restrictive covenant ran with the land.

This is important because *Federated Homes* has not yet been tested in the House of Lords.

Can a positive covenant ever run?

Crow v Wood (1971)	On analogy with this case it has been suggested that a positive covenant involving repair to a fence or hedge forming a boundary between two properties may run. The case itself concerned an easement.

In equity

Although the burden of a restrictive covenant will not run at common law it will run in equity under the rule in *Tulk v Moxhay* (1848) provided the following conditions are met.

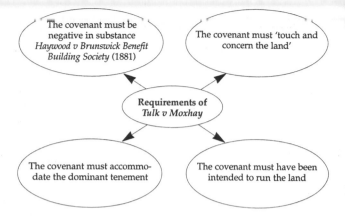

The covenant must be negative in substance
Haywood v Brunswick Benefit Building Society (1881)

The covenant must 'touch and concern the land'

Requirements of
Tulk v Moxhay

The covenant must accommodate the dominant tenement

The covenant must have been intended to run the land

It should be noted that the test for 'touch and concern the land, is the same as that for 'with reference to the subject matter of the lease' for leasehold covenants; that is the test in *Swift Investments*.

Meaning of the covenant must accommodate the dominant tenement	It must confer a benefit on the land retained by the covenantee. At the date the covenant was made the covenantee must have owned the dominant tenement, ie the benefited land: *London Co v Allen* (1914)
The effect of s 79 LPA 1925	If s 79 is interpreted to mean that the covenant will run with the land for all covenants made after 1925, then the covenant will run unless there is a specific term to the contrary

The benefits of restrictive covenants

Again the position must be considered at common law and in equity, although statute is also important in one situation:

The effect of s 56 LPA 1925

This states 'a person may ... take the benefit of any ... covenant ... over or respecting land' although he may not be named as party to the conveyance or other instrument.

This means that someone who is not a party to the covenant may be able to enforce it. Such a person must be:

clearly identifiable

and in existence at the time the covenant was made

The original covenantee can always enforce the covenant for his benefited land because there is always privity of contract between the original parties to the covenant. When either or both covenantee and covenantor has sold land the position needs to be considered both at common law and in equity.

The benefit at common law

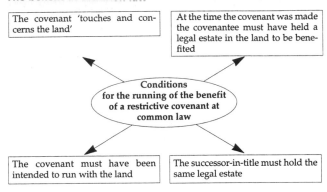

The covenant 'touches and concerns the land'	At the time the covenant was made the covenantee must have held a legal estate in the land to be benefited

Conditions for the running of the benefit of a restrictive covenant at common law

The covenant must have been intended to run with the land	The successor-in-title must hold the same legal estate

Modifications to the conditions as a result of *Smith and Snipes Hall Farm v River Douglas Catchment Board* (1949)

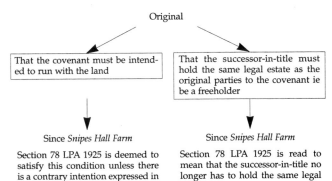

Original

That the covenant must be intended to run with the land	That the successor-in-title must hold the same legal estate as the original parties to the covenant ie be a freeholder

Since *Snipes Hall Farm*

Section 78 LPA 1925 is deemed to satisfy this condition unless there is a contrary intention expressed in the deed

Since *Snipes Hall Farm*

Section 78 LPA 1925 is read to mean that the successor-in-title no longer has to hold the same legal estate, he can be a leaseholder

In equity

Since the burden of a restrictive covenant will only run, if at all, in equity, if it dies then the benefit must also be considered in equity.

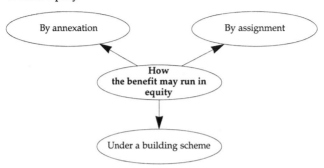

By annexation

Annexation is the attachment of the benefit to the dominant land. This may be done in one of three ways.

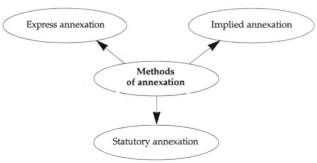

Express annexation requires that the words in the deed expressly state that the benefit of the covenant shall run with the land and clearly identifies that land to be so benefited.

Compare *Renals v Colishaw* (1978) and *Rogers v Hosegood* (1900).

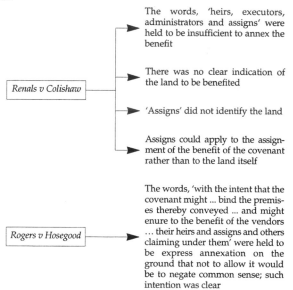

Renals v Colishaw

The words, 'heirs, executors, administrators and assigns' were held to be insufficient to annex the benefit

There was no clear indication of the land to be benefited

'Assigns' did not identify the land

Assigns could apply to the assignment of the benefit of the covenant rather than to the land itself

Rogers v Hosegood

The words, 'with the intent that the covenant might ... bind the premises thereby conveyed ... and might enure to the benefit of the vendors ... their heirs and assigns and others claiming under them' were held to be express annexation on the ground that not to allow it would be to negate common sense; such intention was clear

Note

Even if there are express words and the land is clearly identifiable the courts have not always held there has been annexation: *Re Ballard's Conveyance* (1937). Here the express words were held to benefit part of the land only; the benefit could not run unless the whole estate was involved.

Implied annexation

When circumstances make it clear that there was an intention to annex the benefit to the land, such an intention will be implied as in *Newton Abbot Cooperative Society v Treadgold* (1952).

Annexation by statute

This is the effect of the judgment in *Federated Homes Ltd v Mill Lodge Properties* (1980) when it was held that s 78 served to annex the benefit to the land if the covenant 'touched and concerned the land'. This means that the covenant then runs with the land. This interpretation has been greatly criticised but, as yet, has not been tested in the House of Lords.

Two important cases where s 78 has been considered: *Roake v Chadka* (1984); *Sainsbury v Enfield BC* (1989).

| The application of |
| *Federated Homes* |

Roake v Chadka (1984)

Facts	**The argument**
Land sold to developers with restrictive covenant of only one house per plot. Additional clause: the benefit of the covenant should not run unless the conveyance expressly said it should do so.	The interpretation of s 8 in Federated Homes meant the benefit of the covenant ran with the land so that the owner of a plot could not build a second house on it.

Held: He could build the house. The agreement must be construed as a whole, and the words 'unless the benefit of the restrictive covenant shall be expressly assigned' could not be discounted. There had been no annexation. Section 78 serves to annex the benefit only if there is no contrary expression in the deed.

Sainsbury v Enfield BC (1989)

Facts	Argued
A restrictive covenant made in 1894.	That it was no longer enforceable, so there should be a declaration to that effect.

Held: Section 78 did not apply; the 1989 conveyance had not annexed the benefit to the land. For covenants made before 1925, there must be words which result in express or implied annexation.

By assignment

Where the benefit of a restrictive covenant has not been annexed to the land it may run through express assignment. Assignment is attached to the person holding the benefited land, unlike annexation which attaches to the land itself. This means every time there is a conveyance the land benefit must be assigned.

The following conditions must be satisfied for assignment to be effective:

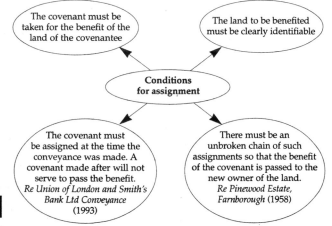

The covenant must be taken for the benefit of the land of the covenantee

The land to be benefited must be clearly identifiable

Conditions for assignment

The covenant must be assigned at the time the conveyance was made. A covenant made after will not serve to pass the benefit. *Re Union of London and Smith's Bank Ltd Conveyance* (1993)

There must be an unbroken chain of such assignments so that the benefit of the covenant is passed to the new owner of the land. *Re Pinewood Estate, Farnborough* (1958)

Building schemes

The benefit of a covenant may be common to several plots of land when they are part of a building scheme.

A developer decides to build an estate

↓

He divides it into plots

↓

He sells the plots and takes a covenant from each buyer

↓

The benefit of these covenants is then transferred to each plot holder and their successors-in-title

↓

This means all owners of houses in the scheme may enforce the covenant and maintain the estate as the developer envisaged

The requirements

A development plan must be in existence before any plot is sold. The plan must show the layout of the plot and the area involved

The developer must be the common vendor for all the plots so that all those buying derive title from this common vendor

Requirements laid down in
Elliston v Reacher
(1908)

Every purchaser must have bought his plot knowing that the covenants were intended to benefit all the plots in the scheme, ie to be mutually binding

Every plot must be subject to the same restrictions at the the plot is sold, and it must be clear that the restrictions were to benefit the whole scheme for all time

Since *Elliston* there have been cases allowing modifications of the scheme.

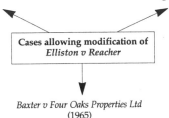

Brunner v Greenslade (1971)

A purchaser of only *part* of a plot was held to be able to enforce a covenant against all the other plot holders in the building scheme.

Re Dolphin's Conveyance (1970)

There was no common vendor, nor a pre-existing plan, before the plots were sold. It was held that there was a common intention when the covenants were taken so that the identical covenants taken by each plot owner were enforceable under a building scheme.

Cases allowing modification of *Elliston v Reacher*

Baxter v Four Oaks Properties Ltd (1965)

A scheme where houses were planned to be of different sizes and prices, but all of which were subject to a covenant restricting them to use as a private dwelling, was allowed.

But note:

Emile Elias v Pine Groves (1993) where a covenant was held not to be enforceable because it was deemed there had been no real building scheme when the estate was first developed.

The modification and discharge of restrictive covenants

Restrictive covenants endure indefinitely, unless they have been discharged, but once terminated they cannot be enforced by anyone; neither by the original covenantee nor his successor-in-title.

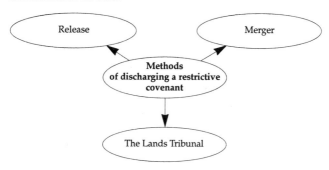

Discharge by release

The only person who can release a restrictive covenant is the person who benefits from it, that is, the covenantee. He may do so in one of two ways.

By express release

This is discharge by deed or by acquiescence, ie by expressly ignoring a breach of covenant. In *Shaw v Applegate* (1978) a property was converted for use as an amusement arcade in contravention of a restrictive covenant. The covenantee had acquiesced to this. The court later refused to grant an injunction to enforce the covenant but did award damages against the original covenantor

By conduct

This is where the court will hold that the covenant was impliedly released because it would be inequitable in the circumstances to enforce it: *Chatsworth Estates v Fewell* (1931).

Discharge by merger

When the two properties, that carrying the burden and that having the benefit of the restrictive covenant, come under one ownership, the covenant is extinguished, the position is comparable to that for easements: *Texaco Antilles Ltd v Kernochan* (1973).

Discharge by the Lands Tribunal

This is governed by s 84(1) of the LPA 1925 which gives the Lands Tribunal a discretion to modify or discharge restrictive covenants, with or without compensation, subject to one of four conditions.

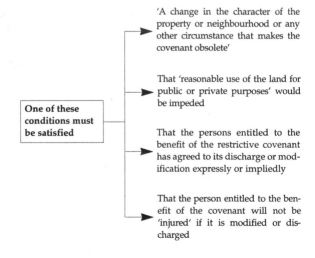

```
                              'A change in the character of the
                              property or neighbourhood or any
                              other circumstance that makes the
                              covenant obsolete'

                              That 'reasonable use of the land for
                              public or private purposes' would
                              be impeded
One of these
conditions must
be satisfied                  That the persons entitled to the
                              benefit of the restrictive covenant
                              has agreed to its discharge or mod-
                              ification expressly or impliedly

                              That the person entitled to the ben-
                              efit of the covenant will not be
                              'injured' if it is modified or dis-
                              charged
```

A person wishing to have the covenant discharged must apply to the tribunal but will, in all cases, have to prove one of the above conditions and that the person entitled to the benefit will be adequately compensated by money.

Discharge is not easily obtained:

Re Beech's Application (1990)

A former council house had been sold with a covenant it should only be used as a dwelling house. Later planning permission was given for use as an office. The Lands Tribunal refused to grant discharge of the covenant

Re Martin's Application (1989)

The court held that a planning decision was not a basis for extinguishing a restrictive covenant

Cases illustrating planning permission and the Lands Tribunal

Re Lloyds and Lloyds Application (1993)

A property was subject to a covenant that it should not be used for trade or business and that no alcohol should be allowed on it. Planning permission was given to make it a community house for psychiatric patients. The house next door had become a building business and there was a home for the aged nearby. The court held that the character of the neighbourhood had changed insufficiently to deem the covenant obsolete but it was government policy to encourage such homes and there was a desperate need for them. The covenant was contrary to this policy and this need. Modification was, therefore, allowed

The protection of restrictive covenants

Registered land

The owner of the benefited land must

Register the covenant against the owner of the burdened land by notice

BUT

before a purchaser buys that burdened land

AND

Notice is only necessary against *a purchaser* of that land. If the burdened land is given as a gift the land remains burdened whether or not the covenant has been registered

If the covenant is not registered it is not enforceable against a purchaser of the burdened land

Unregistered land

The owner of the benefited land must

Register the covenant as a Class D(ii) land charge under the LCA 1972, against the name of the original covenantor

BUT

before the original covenantor sells the land. If this is not done, the covenant will be unenforceable even if the purchaser knew of it before he purchased that land: s 3(6) LCA 1972

AND

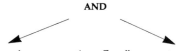

Registration is only necessary for purchasers of the burdened land

For all covenants pre-1026 the doctrine of notice applies

The 1984 Law Commission on Freehold Covenants

This was set up to resolve difficulties and differences in the running of freehold covenants, particularly the fact that the burdens of positive covenants will not run at common law.

Recommendations

An entirely new interest in land to be called a 'land obligation', to be akin to an easement with a dominant land to be benefited and a servient land to be burdened

If the original covenantor transferred his land to a successor-in-title, he should no longer be liable if there were a breach

Land obligations

Either

A 'Neighbour Obligation' which would comprise all existing covenants positive or negative

Or

A 'Development Obligation' where owners of integrated property units shared common obligations and rights

```
                ┌─────────────────────────────┐
                │   Types of land obligations  │
                └─────────────────────────────┘
                       ↙            ↘
```

Legal obligations made by deed, either for a term of years absolute or for a fee simple absolute in possession

Equitable obligations made in writing but not requiring a deed

10 Adverse possession

This is commonly called squatting and is an act of trespass.

The Limitation Act 1980

This governs action that can be taken when someone who has no legal right to land has taken control of it. Under the Act a legal title holder cannot bring an action for the recovery of his land if the person taking it has done so for at least 12 years and done so in a manner that is adverse. After 12 years of adverse possession by another the legal title holder is time-barred from taking action in the courts

Exceptions

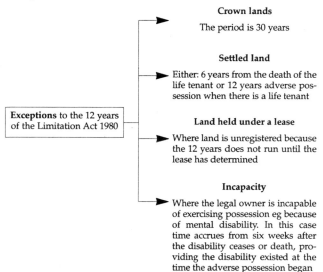

Exceptions to the 12 years of the Limitation Act 1980

Crown lands

The period is 30 years

Settled land

Either: 6 years from the death of the life tenant or 12 years adverse possession when there is a life tenant

Land held under a lease

Where land is unregistered because the 12 years does not run until the lease has determined

Incapacity

Where the legal owner is incapable of exercising possession eg because of mental disability. In this case time accrues from six weeks after the disability ceases or death, providing the disability existed at the time the adverse possession began

Any acknowledgment by the squatter of the legal title holder's right to the land will negate adverse possession

There can be numerous squatters on the land making up the 12 years providing there is a succession of squatters without any gap in time between them *Mount Investments Ltd v Peter Thurlow Ltd* (1988)

The time from which adverse possession begins to accrue

Section 15 of the Limitation Act 1980 and case law determine when adverse possession actually occurs.

In *Wallis Cayton Bay Holiday Camp Ltd v Shell Mex & BP* (1975) it was held to occur when

The true owner had discontinued possession or had been dispossessed

and

the adverse possessor had taken the land adversely ie ouster

In *Treloar v Nute* (1976) the following sufficed:

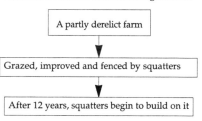

A partly derelict farm

Grazed, improved and fenced by squatters

After 12 years, squatters begin to build on it

Held: The intention was to dispossess the true owner

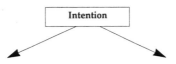

Intention

Of the true owner	**Of the adverse possessor**
If the true owner can prove he intends to use his land there can be no adverse possession: *Leigh v Jack* (1879) when there was an intention to use as a road	He must demonstrate the intention to both dispossess the true owner and to take possession: *Powell v Mcfarlane* (1977) cutting hay, grazing and selling trees from land showed no such intention

Fences as evidence of intention

Putting up a fence has been held to be evidence of *animus possindi* ie intention as in:

Mulcahy v Curramore (1974)

Erection of a fence held to be evidence of occupation by the squatter and 'useful' as signifying his intention to exclude everyone else

and

Sneddon v Smith (1877)

Enclosure held to be the strongest possible evidence of adverse possession

Hughes v Cork (1994)

Enclosure held to be the most cogent evidence of adverse possession and dispossession of the owner

but

Fruin v Fruin (1983)

A fence put up to keep a senile member of the squatter's family in, is not evidence of adverse possession

The Lord-Advocate v Lord Lovat (1888)

per Lord Hagan, 'acts implying possession in one case may be *totally inadequate in another*'

The leading case is *Buckinghamshire County Council v Moran* (1989), in which the whole subject was reviewed.

Moran's land	Narrow strip in between accessible only from Moran's land and in which he planted bulbs	His neighbour's land

It was **held** that Moran had satisfied the conditions for adverse possession that is:

The adverse possessor had evinced an intention to possess the land, but this does not mean of necessity intention to acquire legal title

Possession took place after the true owner had been dispossessed or had abandoned the land and there has been 12 years adverse possession so that the true owner is time-barred from bringing an action for recovery of the land

What happens when the limitation period has expired?

This differs according to whether the land is registered or unregistered.

Unregistered land	Registered land
Under s 17 LA 1980 the title of the paper owner is extinguished	The title of the paper owner is not extinguished; he holds it on trust for the adverse possessor: s 75 LA 1980

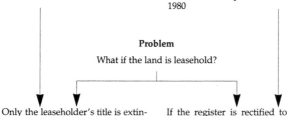

Problem

What if the land is leasehold?

Only the leaseholder's title is extinguished; time does not begin to run against the lease until the lease has come to an end, so that when it determines the freeholder can regain possession: *Fairweather v St Marylebone Property Co Ltd* (1963)	If the register is rectified to give effect to the squatter's interest, then the lessee of the paper title can no longer determine his lease by surrender, so the freeholder cannot regain possession of his land: *Spectrum Investment v Holmes* (1981)

What should the adverse possessor do?

He should seek to register the interest he has now acquired in the land.

If the land is unregistered	If the land is registered
Apply to the Land Registry for registration as proprietor of the land. He will be registered as a proprietor with a possessory title. Where the land is leasehold, registration will be limited to the period of the lease	Apply for rectification of the register under s 82(1) LA 1925. This will give effect to his overriding interest acquired under s 70(1)f LRA 1925. The paper title holder will not be indemnified because the overriding was in existence before the rectification took place: *Re Chowood's Registered Land* (1933

Third party rights

Since an adverse possessor is not a purchaser any third party rights are protected even if they are not registered. They are only void against a purchaser for valuable consideration: *Re Nisbet and Potts Contract* (1906). This means an unregistered covenant can be enforced against an adverse possessor.

There must be no acknowledgment of the paper title holder's legal title

Colchester Borough Council v Smith (1992) seems to extend this to beyond 12 years. A written acknowledgment of such title during negotiations over a dispute after 12 years was ruled to mean the adverse possessor had not satisfied the requirements of s 15 LA 1980.

11 Mortgages

Definitions

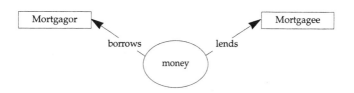

Mortgagor — borrows — money — lends — Mortgagee

Legal mortgages

Legal mortgages of the fee simple absolute in possession, ie freehold s 87 LPA 1925

Either	**Or**
A demise subject to provision for cessor on redemption, which under s 85(2) means there is no transfer of land, but a lease for 3000 years from the start of the mortgage	A charge by way of deed expressed by way of legal mortgage s 87

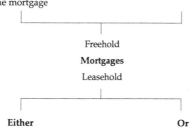

Freehold

Mortgages

Leasehold

Either	**Or**
A legal mortgage under a sub-lease at least 10 days shorter than the unexpired lease with provision for cessor	A charge by way of deed expressed to be by way of legal mortgage

Legal mortgages for a term of years absolute, ie of leases

Equitable mortgages

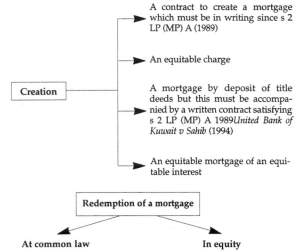

Creation	▶	A contract to create a mortgage which must be in writing since s 2 LP (MP) A (1989)
	▶	An equitable charge
	▶	A mortgage by deposit of title deeds but this must be accompanied by a written contract satisfying s 2 LP (MP) A 1989 *United Bank of Kuwait v Sahib* (1994)
	▶	An equitable mortgage of an equitable interest

Redemption of a mortgage

At common law

At the date given in the contract, neither earlier nor later

In equity

To redeem on reasonable terms, even if this is not the date in the contract

The rights of the mortgagor ie the equity of redemption which is the total bundle of rights and not just the equitable right to redeem

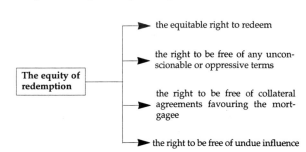

The equity of redemption	▶	the equitable right to redeem
	▶	the right to be free of any unconscionable or oppressive terms
	▶	the right to be free of collateral agreements favouring the mortgagee
	▶	the right to be free of undue influence

The equitable right to redeem
'Once a mortgage, always a mortgage.'

This maxim means a mortgage can never be anything else, so anything which makes redemption illusory will be void. This means there can be:

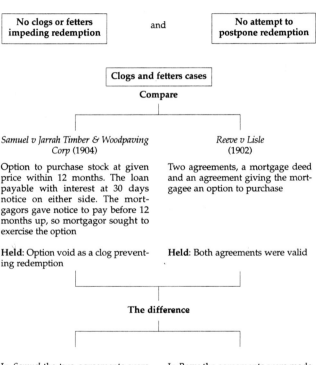

| No clogs or fetters impeding redemption | and | No attempt to postpone redemption |

Clogs and fetters cases

Compare

Samuel v Jarrah Timber & Woodpaving Corp (1904)	*Reeve v Lisle* (1902)
Option to purchase stock at given price within 12 months. The loan payable with interest at 30 days notice on either side. The mortgagors gave notice to pay before 12 months up, so mortgagor sought to exercise the option	Two agreements, a mortgage deed and an agreement giving the mortgagee an option to purchase
Held: Option void as a clog preventing redemption	**Held**: Both agreements were valid

The difference

| In *Samuel* the two agreements were made together so the mortgagor could have felt he would not have the mortgage if he did not accept the option agreement | In *Reeve* the agreements were made 10 days apart so no clog on the equity of redemption |

Redemption illusory: cases

Knightsbridge Estates Trust Ltd v Byrne (1940)	*Fairclough v Swan Brewery Co Ltd* (1912)
A 40 year mortgage with a clause that one default in the repayment of instalments would mean principal sum and interest payable immediately. The mortgagor sought to redeem to take out a cheaper mortgage	A mortgage on leasehold property with 17½ years to run of a 20 year lease. A clause prevented redemption until six weeks before lease expired
Held: He could not	**Held**: In practice an irredeemable mortgage

The right to be free of oppressive or unconscionable terms

Unconscionable does not mean unreasonable but morally reprehensible. A high interest rate is not necessarily oppressive. As the following cases illustrate it depends on the circumstances.

Cityland and Property (Holdings) Ltd v Dabrah (1986)

Tenant to be evicted when
lease expired sought to buy freehold

↓

Landlord provided money for purchase
by a 'premium' instead of a rate of interest

↓

Premium turned out to be
equivalent to an interest rate of 12%

Held: The agreement was unconscionable; 7% would have been fair; the parties were not equal in bargaining power

Multiservice Bookbinding Ltd v Marden (1979)

Mortgage taken in terms of the Swiss franc

$\downarrow$

Swiss franc jumps in value against the pound sterling

$\downarrow$

Are mortgage terms now oppressive?

Held: No; it was a perfectly legal agreement

Note
Mortgage terms related to other criteria such as index-linked repayments or PEPS which may mean heavy increases in repayments, depending on rises in inflation or depression in share values, are also not regarded as unconscionable or oppressive

The right to be free of disadvantageous collateral agreements
This means the mortgagee must not make terms that give him another advantage, for example, by insisting on an agreement which prevents the mortgagor from organising his business as he wishes.

The court's attitude to such agreements was very strict in the old cases but has tended to be more liberal in the last half-century, and looked at the bargaining position of the parties.

In all cases where the restrictions placed by the mortgagee have been limited to the mortgage term the courts have been less likely to rule the agreements void.

Biggs v Hodinott (1898)

A 5 year mortgage restricting mortgagor to buying beer only from the mortgagor during the mortgage and no redemption possible for 5 years

Held: The 5 year term was reasonable

Noakes v Rice (1902)

The mortgage clause restricted the mortgagor, the lessee of a public house, to buying beer from the mortgagee alone, not only for the term of the mortgage but for the whole term of the lease

Held: This infringed the maxim 'once a mortgage, always a mortgage'.

Collateral agreements

Kreglinger v New Patagonia Meat & Cold Storage Co Ltd (1914)

A mortgage was attached to an agreement that the mortgagor meat company would offer its sheepskins to the mortgagees for five years, and who, if they wished, would buy them at market price

Held: The option was valid; the 5 years term was reasonable and the purchase of skins was at market price. The option and the mortgage were separate agreements.

Esso Petroleum Co Ltd v Harper's Garage (Southport) Ltd (1968)

An agreement for the exclusive supply of petrol for 21 years collateral to a mortgage agreement for 21 years was held to be void but one for 5 years for a second garage held to be reasonable

More modern cases

Alec Lobb Garages Ltd v Total Oil GB Ltd (1985)

Reaffirmed that the crucial factor is the length of time the agreement is to last; five year is reasonable

The right to be free of undue influence

Where there is more than one legal owner of property and one of them wishes to mortgage it, all the legal title holders will be required to sign the mortgage deed.

In such a case it sometimes happens that the other, or others are persuaded to sign in such a manner as to raise the possibility of undue influence having been exerted. Where this is proven the courts have often found against the mortgagee.

The position was reviewed and reconsidered in the following landmark cases:

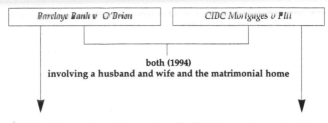

| *Barclays Bank v O'Brien* | *CIBC Mortgages v Pitt* |

both (1994)
involving a husband and wife and the matrimonial home

W signed the mortgage document and the accompanying letter stating that she had been told what was involved. She did not read either. She thought that the money involved was limited and was not to cover the debts of a company her H was associated with

H obtained a mortgage by telling the finance company he wanted to pay off his existing mortgage. H persuaded his W to agree with the lie. He in fact wanted it to buy shares. The shares later collapsed in value and the mortgagees sought possession of the house

The House of Lords decisions

The mortgage could not be enforced against W

The mortgage was enforceable against W

It is clear that in cases where there is more than one legal owner of property and there is a relationship between them that could give rise to a situation of undue influence the mortgagee has a duty make to sure that such person or persons receive independent advice.

Failure to do so may mean the mortgagee will be seen as having constructive notice of such influence and thereby deemed to have exerted it himself.

Where the mortgagee has advised independent advice he has been allowed possession. Recent cases illustrate this:

INDEPENDENT ADVICE

TSB v Camfield (1995)

A wife agreed to a mortgage of the matrimonial home when her husband told her it was for £15,000 only. Her H had made a genuine mistake: the actual amount was unlimited. The bank asked its own solicitors to ensure W received independent advice. The solicitors said this had been done but had only seen her with H

Held: W had been innocently misled and had not received independent advice so the bank had constructive notice of H's inducement to obtain her consent

Massey v Midland Bank (1995)

A lover (but not a cohabitee) obtained a mortgage on his mistress' house by purporting to obey the bank's instruction to make sure she obtained independent advice before signing the mortgage documents. He took her to see his own solicitor and remained in the room while the situation was explained to her.

Held: The bank had been put on enquiry but were entitled to believe their advice had been taken. They were not required to know all the details of the meeting when it was explained to the mistress.

The rights of the mortgagee

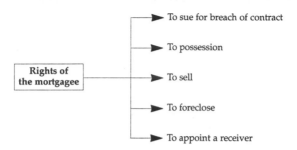

- To sue for breach of contract
- To possession
- To sell
- To foreclose
- To appoint a receiver

Rights of the mortgagee

The right of possession

This exists 'before the ink is dry on the paper': *Four Maids Ltd v Dudley Marsh* (1957) unless there is a contrary clause in the mortgage deed.

Possession is usually sought as a preliminary to sale. If there is no sale the mortgagee may find himself having to account for any money he has, or should have received.

Authority: *White City v City of London Brewery* (1889).

Possession requires a court order: *Quennell v Maltby* (1979).

Possession when a dwelling house is involved

The court in this case has other powers under s 36 of the 1970 Act as amended by the AJA 1973.

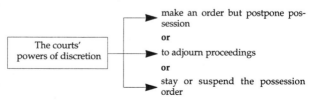

The courts' powers of discretion

- make an order but postpone possession

  or

- to adjourn proceedings

  or

- stay or suspend the possession order

The court in exercising its discretion will look at whether there is a reasonable chance that the mortgagor will be able to pay the arrears in a reasonable time: *Target Home Loans v Clothier* (1994).

Since the 1973 Act it is no longer necessary for the principal sum to be paid as well as the arrears.

The right to sell the mortgaged property

This arises as soon as one instalment is due but unpaid: *Payne v Cardiff* (1932). Sale is governed by s 101 of the LPA 1925.

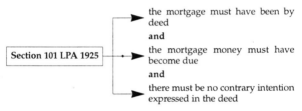

```
                          the mortgage must have been by
                          deed
                          and
 Section 101 LPA 1925     the mortgage money must have
                          become due
                          and
                          there must be no contrary intention
                          expressed in the deed
```

The power of sale cannot be exercised until the requirements of s 103 are met.

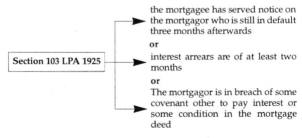

```
                          the mortgagee has served notice on
                          the mortgagor who is still in default
                          three months afterwards
                          or
 Section 103 LPA 1925     interest arrears are of at least two
                          months
                          or
                          The mortgagor is in breach of some
                          covenant other to pay interest or
                          some condition in the mortgage
                          deed
```

Should the mortgagee sell before meeting the requirements of s 101 and s 103, the mortgagor may sue him for damages.

The mortgagee has also other duties:

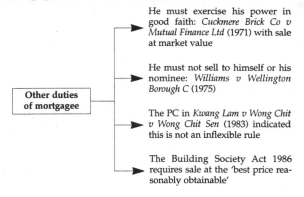

Other duties of mortgagee

He must exercise his power in good faith: *Cuckmere Brick Co v Mutual Finance Ltd* (1971) with sale at market value

He must not sell to himself or his nominee: *Williams v Wellington Borough C* (1975)

The PC in *Kwang Lam v Wong Chit v Wong Chit Sen* (1983) indicated this is not an inflexible rule

The Building Society Act 1986 requires sale at the 'best price reasonably obtainable'

The mortgagee must use the proceeds of sale in accordance with s 105 of the LPA 1925.

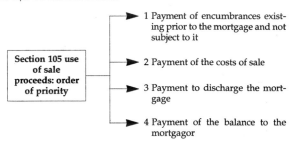

Section 105 use of sale proceeds: order of priority

1 Payment of encumbrances existing prior to the mortgage and not subject to it

2 Payment of the costs of sale

3 Payment to discharge the mortgage

4 Payment of the balance to the mortgagor

The mortgagors were in a negative equity situation and the mortgagee objected to their selling because there would still be a debt. The mortgagee wanted to rent out the house and sell when prices improved

Held: The court had a complete discretion to order a sale even if mortgagor did not wish it

Halifax Building Society v Thomas
(1995)

A mortgagee with a possession order sold the property. There was the property. There was a balance which he put in his own account on grounds that it was a profit on a mortgage obtained by fraud

Held: The money was held for the mortgagor in accordance with s 105

Two important cases

The mortgagee's right to foreclose

This is virtually a right to confiscate the property of the mortgagor. It requires a court order and is rarely used. Such an order is only obtainable if:

The legal date of
redemption has passed

and

A court action is
undertaken

The mortgagee's right to appoint a receiver

This is given by s 109 LPA 1925.

Note

Lloyds Bank plc v Bryant (1996). A mortgagee has no duty to the mortgagor to exercise his power to sell etc in a positive way. Even if the receivers mismanage the property there is no recourse from the mortgagee. The receiver is the agent of the mortgagor only.

Co-ownership and implied consent to a mortgage

Implied consent is deemed to exist where a person holding the legal title has taken out a mortgage without objection from another who has an equitable interest in the property.

A refusal, by the person claiming an interest in the property, and in occupation, to state such an interest when the mortgagee makes enquiries. Such a person will be estopped from exerting such interest against a mortgagee or a purchaser: *Midland Bank Ltd v Farmpride Properties Ltd* (1992)

A person who knows that the legal title holder is mortgaging a property in which he or she has an interest and allows it will be deemed to have given consent and will be estopped from exerting such interest: *Paddington Building Society v Mendlesohn* (1985)

Situations of implied consent

Where a person having a beneficial interest in a property has consented to a mortgage on it, such person will be held to have impliedly agreed to the legal title holder taking out a second mortgage on it, even though they neither knew of, nor consented to, this second mortgage. This means the second mortgagee steps into the shoes of the first mortgagee, and in the case of default the second mortgagee takes priority over that person's interest. This was established in *Equity and Law Home Loans v Prestidge* (1992)

The protection and priority of mortgages

The position must be considered separately for registered and unregistered land.

Registered land

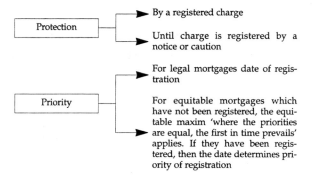

Protection
- By a registered charge
- Until charge is registered by a notice or caution

Priority
- For legal mortgages date of registration
- For equitable mortgages which have not been registered, the equitable maxim 'where the priorities are equal, the first in time prevails' applies. If they have been registered, then the date determines priority of registration

Unregistered land

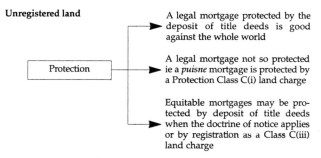

Protection
- A legal mortgage protected by the deposit of title deeds is good against the whole world
- A legal mortgage not so protected ie a *puisne* mortgage is protected by a Protection Class C(i) land charge
- Equitable mortgages may be protected by deposit of title deeds when the doctrine of notice applies or by registration as a Class C(iii) land charge

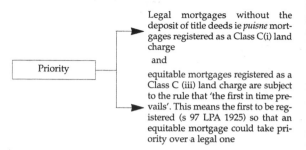

Priority

Legal mortgages without the deposit of title deeds ie *puisne* mortgages registered as a Class C(i) land charge

and

equitable mortgages registered as a Class C (iii) land charge are subject to the rule that 'the first in time prevails'. This means the first to be registered (s 97 LPA 1925) so that an equitable mortgage could take priority over a legal one

There is a problem where there are several *puisne* mortgages, because there appears to be a conflict between s 97 LPA 1925 and s 4(5) LCA 1972.

Problem

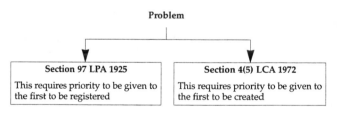

Section 97 LPA 1925	**Section 4(5) LCA 1972**
This requires priority to be given to the first to be registered	This requires priority to be given to the first to be created

Example

Order of events:

Ann creates a *puisne* mortgage

Victor creates a *puisne* mortgage

Ann registers her mortgage

Victor registers his mortgage

Who has priority?
According to

Section 97 LPA 1925	Section 4(5) LCA 1972
Ann because her charge was created before Victor registered his charge.	Victor because Ann had not registered hers before Victor's was created

This conflict remains.

The Law Commission Report on mortgages of land

The Commission's report resulted in a draft bill in 1991. It recommended:

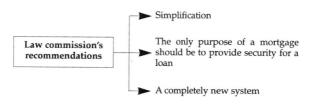

Law commission's recommendations
- Simplification
- The only purpose of a mortgage should be to provide security for a loan
- A completely new system

The proposed system

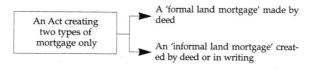

An Act creating two types of mortgage only
- A 'formal land mortgage' made by deed
- An 'informal land mortgage' created by deed or in writing

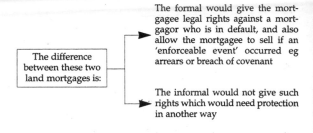

The difference between these two land mortgages is:

The formal would give the mortgagee legal rights against a mortgagor who is in default, and also allow the mortgagee to sell if an 'enforceable event' occurred eg arrears or breach of covenant

The informal would not give such rights which would need protection in another way

Both would cover legal and equitable interests but the mortgagee would no longer have a right to possession. However the court would grant possession if the property was to be sold. The court would also have power to vary the mortgage terms if it thought it equitable to do so.